D1685429

This book is to be returned on
or before the date stamped below

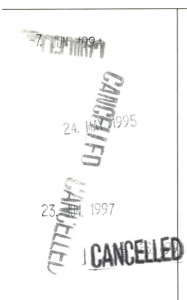

-7. JUN 1994

CANCELLED

24. MAY 1995

CANCELLED

14. OCT 1999

23. JAN. 1997

-3. FEB 1999

CANCELLED

CANCELLED

UNIVERSITY OF PLYMOUTH

ACADEMIC SERVICES
PLYMOUTH LIBRARY
Tel: (0752) 232323
This book is subject to recall if required by another reader
Books may be renewed by phone
CHARGES WILL BE MADE FOR OVERDUE BOOKS

Dealing With Whitehall

For
Jeanne, Ruth and Andrew

Dealing
With
Whitehall

Philip Connelly

CENTURY
BUSINESS

First published in Great Britain in 1992 by
Century Business
An imprint of Random House UK Limited
20 Vauxhall Bridge Road, London SW1V 2SA

Random House Australia (Pty) Limited
20 Alfred Street, Milsons Point, Sydney
New South Wales 2061, Australia

Random House New Zealand Limited
18 Poland Road, Glenfield
Auckland 10, New Zealand

Random House South Africa (Pty) Limited
PO Box 337, Bergvlei, South Africa

Set in Bembo by Edna A Moore ᴁ\ Tek-Art, Addiscombe, Croydon, Surrey

British Library Cataloguing in Publication Data
A catalogue record for this book is available from the British Library

ISBN 0-7126-5060-1

Companies, institutions and other organizations wishing to make bulk purchases of this title or any other Century Business publication should contact:

Direct Sales Manager
Century Business
Random Century House
20 Vauxhall Bridge Road
London SW1V 2SA

Fax: 071-828 6681

Contents

PART III LOBBYING PARLIAMENT

PART IV THE PRESSURE GROUPS

PART V WHITEHALL IN ACTION

APPENDICES

Part I

Setting the Scene

1
The Impact
of Government

Every business, large or small, feels the impact of government. Apart from the overarching performance of government with regard to inflation, interest and exchange rates, etc., many particular official measures bear directly on business. At the most basic level, perhaps, government levies taxes. In addition to those which apply generally to all companies, such as Corporation Tax or Value Added Tax, there are several taxes specially designed to deal with individual industries, such as Petroleum Revenue Tax in the offshore oil and gas industry, the Special Car Tax on new cars, or the Exchequer Levy on Independent Television company revenues.

The most comprehensive role of government in relation to business is that of a regulator, imposing rules affecting the whole range of a company's operations. Employment law governs the recruitment of staff; health and safety legislation regulates their conditions of work. Company law affects the corporate structure of the business, and prescribes the duties of company directors. Competition law puts limits on market dominance, while hosts of detailed consumer protection regulations cover labelling and packaging, advertising and food hygiene, and much more. As with taxation, there are special regulatory regimes for particular industries or sectors, e.g., food or broadcasting or nuclear energy.

Governments also have a positive role. Even those administrations which espouse non-interventionist principles do, in practice, take decisions and adopt policies which change the business landscape. The various privatization and liberalization measures carried out by the Conservative Government since 1979 have created new businesses and new opportunities for those and other businesses, e.g., the direct sale of electricity by generators to industrial customers, or the ability of new entrants to enter commercial television by bidding for franchises. Again, governments of all complexions take steps to encourage inward investment, but often attach conditions. In the case of incoming Japanese vehicle assemblers, the Conservative Government negotiated detailed Memoranda of Understanding with these companies on the 'local content' targets which they should aim for in their components purchasing. A similar policy with regard to the purchasing arrangements of foreign oil companies operating in the North Sea was initiated by a Labour Government and continued by a succeeding Conservative administration.

Furthermore, the Conservative Government since 1979 has evolved a whole battery of initiatives, involving not inconsiderable sums of public money, designed to improve the competitiveness of British industry. Information, advice, grants, subsidies, loan guarantees, secondments, etc., all form part of the repertoire. Still further, businesses have been brought by government into the task of urban regeneration, of improving youth and adult training, and much else besides. In real life, there is no such thing as a 'hands-off' government as far as business is concerned.

Government has, of course, a most important commercial dimension. It is a customer of business on a vast scale. The National Health Service, for example, spends £4 billion per annum on supplies. But the biggest single customer of British business, by a wide margin, is the Ministry of Defence. Its 37,000 strong Procurement Executive places around £8 billion worth of orders every year to defence contractors and their enormous network of suppliers. Its policies and practices in that vast purchasing programme have an enormous influence on the health of several industries, especially electronics. Similarly, the government is the biggest user of information technology in the country. While individual departments and agencies increasingly take their own decisions with regard to the procurement of IT, the Central Computing and Telecommunications Agency (part of the Treasury) has for many years occupied a pivotal position, as procurer or adviser, between departments and the IT industry. In competing internationally, many defence and IT contractors will feel disadvantaged if they are unable to point to orders from their home government.

Finally, though successive privatizations have greatly reduced the size of the public sector in its role as a supplier to business, the Government still has substantial and continuing operations, for example, in the provision of road transport infrastructure – vitally important in an economy where more than nine out of 10 passengers and more than eight out of every 10 tonnes of freight travel by road. Some would say that the most vital supplier role of government is that of well-educated entrants to the workforce.

It would be labouring the point to produce further examples of the impact of government on business. Its influence is all-pervasive. Business therefore needs to be aware of the activities of government; and to understand the decision-taking process of government and how to participate in it. That is the purpose of this book. The need for a book arises from the fact that the process of government is seriously under-reported by the media and therefore is badly understood by many businesspeople. If this is true of the UK domestic scene, the problem is exacerbated by the increasingly important part played by European Community (EC) institutions and their interaction with the British system. EC institutions and procedures are briefly described in the next chapter.

It would be wrong to suggest that there is a complete communications failure between government and business, but the situation is rather patchy. Government departments and agencies do indeed devote significant resources to disseminating information to the public and the media about their activities. However most of this effort is devoted to announcing programmes; that is, explaining the outcomes of decisions rather than how they were made. A handful of journalists in the quality press keep a watching eye on Whitehall, but the space allocated to them by their editors is modest, and their government canvas includes social policy, education, etc., which are often deemed more newsworthy than business. Some of the biggest companies in the country, like BP, ICI, etc., have in-house staff whose task is to study the workings of government, Parliament, pressure groups, etc., and brief their colleagues accordingly. Such companies are, however, in a small minority and, of course, the knowledge thus gained stays for the most part within the companies and does not raise the general level of understanding. There are a number of consultancies – both firms and individuals – offering services variously described as 'public affairs', 'government relations' or 'parliamentary consultancy'. They vary greatly in the scope and quality of the service provided. All can provide basic information on government and Parliament; most can arrange parliamentary contacts and assistance with lobbying in Parliament. A few know their way around Whitehall and fewer still understand the interactions between Westminster, Whitehall, the media, pressure groups and the European Community.

The most generally available and widely used means of communication between business and government are trade associations. Undoubtedly, a well-resourced trade association, employing good quality staff, representative of its sector and enjoying the enthusiastic participation of its membership at a senior level, can perform a vital communications function with government. Sadly, the reality often falls short of the potential. Britain probably has too many trade associations, none of them really adequately funded and therefore unable to recruit and retain the best staff. Member companies complain about subscription levels while failing to make the link between resources and effective representation. Nor do they encourage their best people to play an active part in the work of the organizations. This is not to deny the good work which is done in the trade association network, but a much higher quality of communications would flow from rationalization and increased support, through both finance and participation.

Therefore the businessman who seeks to understand the governmental decision-making process as it affects his company, and to play a part in it, needs to devote a little effort to the task. This book is designed to make that task easier.

2
The European
Context

INTRODUCTION

British industry exports over £100 million worth of goods to other EC
countries every day; half of all UK trade is with the EC. The Community's
population is already approaching that of the USA and Japan combined,
and other applications for membership (Sweden, Austria) are in the
pipeline. The European Free Trade Association (EFTA) came to an
agreement with the EC in October 1991 for a common economic zone,
subject to parliamentary ratification. The policies and procedures of the EC
as they affect British business are therefore of outstanding importance.
Today, British business needs to know how to lobby Brussels as well as
Whitehall. The two are different. The EC inevitably presents a more
complex decision-making process, reflecting not only the interplay between
Brussels and individual member governments, but also the special role
given to the Commission, which is quite different to that of a national civil
service.

It is beyond the scope of this book to describe in any detail the EC
system as well as that of the UK. However, EC work is now the daily
bread of Whitehall's departments, UK trade associations, pressure groups,
etc., and once the operations of the latter are understood, several entry
points into the EC system will be identified. As background, this chapter
describes some basic features of EC institutions and procedures, the
particular relevance of the 1992 project to complete the Single Market and
the contact points for lobbying the EC. Appendix A gives the names and
addresses of a range of EC and other organizations from which further
information may be obtained.

To be effective, lobbying in Brussels has to match the complexity of the decision-making process. You will need to communicate with several institutions, all of which are involved in an interactive, bargaining process. On the other hand, there is something of a Washington-type atmosphere; the inhabitants of official Brussels know that they are there, amongst other things, to listen to representations, are accustomed to it and are generally open and receptive. As in all dealings with officialdom, go prepared. If you wish to lobby Brussels yourself, go first of all to your trade association and the relevant UK government department for a briefing and to establish who is dealing with, or interested in, the subject in the Commission, Parliament and UKREP (the UK Government's permanent representation in Brussels, see below). Your own Member of the European Parliament (MEP) may also be able to help. He can be contacted through the UK constituency office. Details of MEPs are usually available in public libraries, or through the European Parliament Information Office in London.

There are five types of EC legislation:

- *Regulations* are the strictest form; they are directly applicable in all member states and need no further legislative process in the member states in order to be fully binding
- *Directives* are binding as to the objectives, but leave it to the member states to enact domestically the means for the objectives to be achieved, while imposing a time limit for that to be done
- *Decisions* are directly binding; they are specific administrative acts performed under the authority of Community legislation, e.g., when the Commission imposes a fine on a company found to be in breach of EC competition law
- *Recommendations and Opinions*, while formal instruments, are not binding

The main formal EC Institutions are: the Commission, the Council of Ministers, the European Parliament and the European Court of Justice. In broadest terms, the Commission makes proposals; the Parliament gives opinions on and suggests amendments to those proposals; the Council of Ministers decides; and the Court interprets the treaties upon which the EC is based and generally makes judgments on matters of EC law.

The formal decision-making methodology used by the Council is important. Each proposal put to the Council for ultimate decision is based on an article of one of the treaties upon which the Community is founded, and these provide, variously, for three voting bases for decisions: unanimous, simple majority and qualified (i.e. weighted) majority. As we shall see later, the Single European Act 1987 greatly extended the use of qualified majority votes which has had a marked impact on the productivity of EC legislation.

THE COMMISSION

The Commission has 17 members nominated by member states for four-yearly renewable terms, increasing to five years in 1995. Two come from each of the larger member states and one from each of the smaller. Once in post, they swear to act in the EC interest, not that of their home country. In practice, of course, it is not in the nature of human beings, far less politicians, totally to forswear any sympathy with their home base. At the time of writing; the two British Commissioners and their areas of responsibility are:

Sir Leon Brittan (Competition Policy, Financial Institutions)
Bruce Millan (Regional Policy)

The staff of the Commission, recruited from all member countries, are organized into 23 directorates-general, e.g., DG IV – Competition, DG III – Internal Market and Industrial Affairs, plus some service departments. Although often castigated as a bloated bureaucracy, the Commission staff of 13,000 is comparable to that of a London Borough Council. (See Appendix B for list of directorates-general and their component directorates.) The Commission publishes its own directory, giving details of directorates and names of officials.

The main tasks of the Commission are to:

- Propose EC policy and legislation. It alone has the right of initiating proposals to the Council of Ministers
- Implement EC decisions and policies
- Ensure that member states comply with EC rules

The Commission is not a European version of a UK civil service working in support of UK ministers. It is proactive; an institution in its own right, with powers unheard of in Whitehall, including certain decision-making powers in addition to the pivotal right to initiate legislation. It maintains an international network of offices (in the UK, in Belfast,

Cardiff, Edinburgh and London). It is, in many ways, an outward-looking organization. Dealing with it, however, can tend to lend credence to the accusations of bureaucracy. It can be slow; there is much referral up the chain of command; its documentation is voluminous and the contents may often seem stilted. In fairness, however, such characteristics must inevitably attach to an organization which deals with 12 member states, works in nine official languages and has an international staff. You may deal with a German case officer reporting to a French head of division under an Italian director general.

In making representations to the Commission, as with Whitehall, you should start with the case officer, that is the administrative official actually doing the work of analysing, consulting, drafting and recommending. In the UK civil service this would be around grade 7; the Brussels equivalent is not so clear-cut, between grades A5–A7.

Depending on the nature of the subject, and on the reading of the situation you will gain from your circuit of all the organizations and institutions involved, you may need to contact a commissioner, either one responsible for the directorate general concerned, or possibly a British commissioner. This should be done only after taking advice, and through his 'cabinet' – a group of advisers usually recruited from the commissioner's home country and roughly equivalent to a UK minister's private office.

The members of the cabinet perform an important role in organizing the work of the commissioners. They help to resolve issues between other cabinets rather than have the commissioners consider all the details at their formal weekly meetings when decisions are taken by simple majority vote. It may therefore be appropriate to contact the member of the cabinet responsible for the subject which concerns you, without always needing to seek a meeting with the commissioner.

The Commission is itself proactive in discussing its proposals in draft form with business. Its inclination is naturally to consult those organizations which can claim to be representative of business in the EC. It will also consult with civil servants from member countries. This consultative stage is vital for you to penetrate. It is here that unrealistic notions can be challenged and withdrawn before they become proposals. Information and research can be input. In particular, all Commission proposals for legislation must be accompanied by an impact statement (*fiche d'impact*) assessing the impact on business of the proposals. It is up to business to ensure that this statement is realistic. The way to do that is, as in Whitehall, through a full and effective participation in the consultative network of trade associations and government officials. The difference in Brussels is, of course, the need to produce evidence that businesses in other member countries are with you in your representations.

THE COUNCIL OF MINISTERS

The Council is the ultimate decision taking body of the EC. Each member state has a seat on the council, but the individual occupying the seat varies according to the subject being discussed, e.g., agriculture, environment etc., when the appropriate departmental ministers attend.

Foreign ministers meeting in Council oversee the others and twice a year the heads of state or government meet to discuss broad areas of policy – the 'European Summit'. Council meetings, of which there are some 90 per year, are chaired by the representative of the member stage occupying the presidency. This rotates every six months, in alphabetical order of member states.

All EC member states have a representative office in Brussels staffed by civil servants, the most senior of whom in each case has ambassador status. The collective body of these offices is known as COREPER (Committee of Permanent Representatives) and plays a vital role in permanent negotiation between member states on the position to be taken on Commission proposals. Normally, Commission proposals will be considered first by a working group of officials from member states before going to COREPER.

The job of co-ordinating the work of Council meetings falls to COREPER, in conjunction with the Secretariat of the Council. The work is far from administrative in nature; in practice, COREPER negotiates and decides on a great mass of issues which therefore either do not need to come up for decision at Council or can be dealt with there expeditiously. COREPER is part of the decision-making system. The British permanent representation, known as UKREP, is staffed by civil servants seconded from various Whitehall departments, plus the Foreign Office, which takes the lead. These officials know what is going on in Brussels and provide the link both with Whitehall and with their opposite numbers in the offices of other member countries. Your first port of call in Brussels should probably be with the UKREP desk officer dealing with the issue which concerns you. Your trade association or UK government department will tell you who he is, or you may contact UKREP direct.

EUROPEAN PARLIAMENT

The European Parliament has 518 Members (MEPs), 81 from the UK, directly elected for a fixed five-year term. They have formed into, and sit as, some ten political groupings rather than national delegations. As is well known, the Parliament has no permanent home: committee meetings are held in Brussels and monthly plenary sessions in Strasbourg, with the Secretariat mostly based in Luxembourg.

The opinion of the Parliament must be given to most Commission proposals before they can be adopted by the Council of Ministers and become law. Under the Single European Act, as we shall see, this role has been strengthened.

The work of the European Parliament is based upon committees. There are 18 specialist subject standing committees, each with a permanent secretariat. Unlike the departmental select committees of the UK Parliament, they usually conflate several subjects into their titles. The five committees of primary interest to business are:

- Economic and Monetary Affairs
- Energy, Research and Technology
- Social Affairs, Employment and the Working Environment
- Transport and Tourism
- Environment, Public Health and Consumer Protection

When the Commission sends a proposal to Parliament, it is referred immediately to one (or sometimes more) of these committees. In turn, the committee appoints a 'rapporteur' – one of its members – who examines the proposal, proposes amendments to the committee, presents the committee's report to Parliament and sees it through the subsequent stages of legislation; which usually involves negotiations with the Commission and the Council. Depending on the treaty article under which the Commission's proposal is invoked, either the Consultation or Co-operation Procedure is followed.

The 'rapporteur', his personal research assistant if he has one, and the responsible official in the secretariat of the standing committee are, evidently, important targets for lobbying if the subject being dealt with impacts upon your business. More generally, as in Westminster, the political groupings have their subject specialists, and there are various all-party groups, all of whom may need to figure in your communications programme.

A new lease of life – the Single European Act

Many people in business will have the jaundiced memories of EC proposals affecting their industries taking years to work their way through EC institutions, and often then coming to a halt due to a veto by a member country. There was indeed a period of growing frustration with the EC system which built up during the 1970s and early 1980s. Classic stories were quoted widely, e.g., of the directive on lawnmower noise which took six years to reach agreement. The log-jam of frustrations experienced by many in European industry was broken by the accession of Jacques Delors to the Presidency of the European Commission and the appointment of Lord Cockfield, previously UK Secretary of State for Trade, as Commissioner responsible for the internal market portfolio. It was Lord Cockfield who enunciated the principle that a truly Common Market without internal barriers would only come about if all the requisite measures were set out comprehensively with a deadline imposed for their implementation. Thus was '1992' born.

In the event, some 280 measures needed to complete the internal market were identified and set out in a Commission White Paper in 1985. This covered physical and fiscal barriers (e.g., customs and VAT checks); and also technical barriers. This covers an extremely wide range of matters of direct concern to all sectors of business, e.g., safety standards, public procurement, recognition of qualifications, financial services, transport, intellectual property and many more. The White Paper also set out the timetable target – 1992 – by which the measures had to be implemented. It took a further two years from the publication of the White Paper for all EC member states to commit themselves formally to the internal market programme, through ratification of the Single European Act (SEA).

The SEA is the name given to a parcel of amendments to the Treaty of Rome, in other words, a set of constitutional reforms of the EC necessary to give effect to the completion of the internal market. The main changes were as follows.

- *Majority voting rather than unanimity*. No longer can a member state veto a measure (unless it has to do with certain prescribed non-internal market measures: tax, movement of people and conditions of employment). For internal market subjects, therefore, the voting

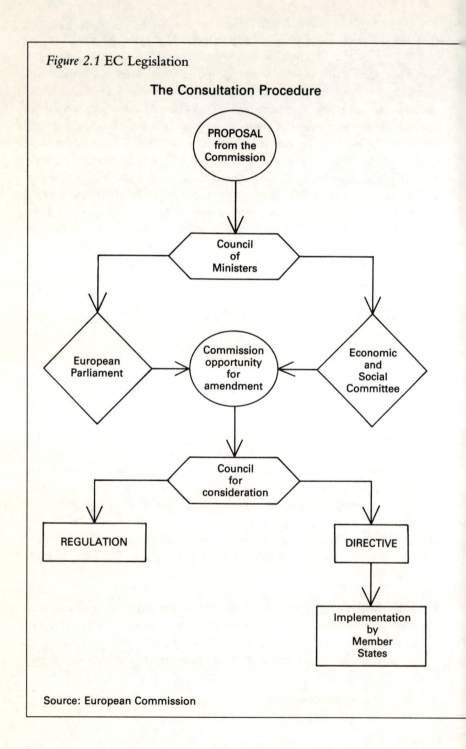

Figure 2.1 EC Legislation

The Consultation Procedure

Source: European Commission

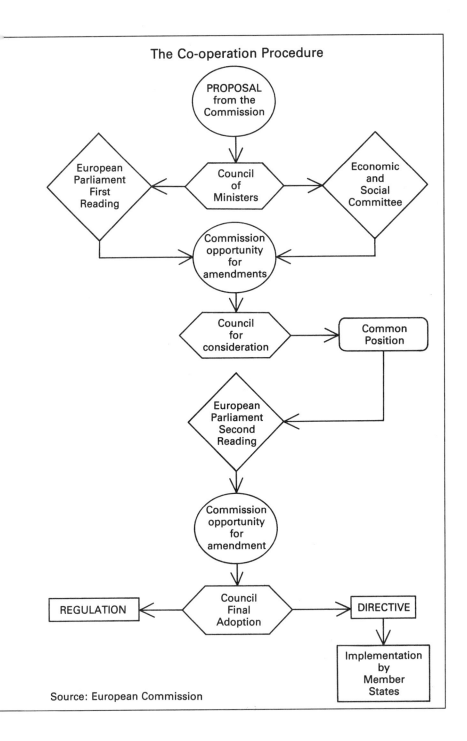

The Co-operation Procedure

Source: European Commission

system is a qualified majority, based on votes weighted according to the member country's population:

	Votes
Germany	10
France	10
UK	10
Italy	10
Spain	8
Holland	5
Belgium	5
Greece	5
Portugal	5
Ireland	3
Denmark	3
Luxembourg	2
	76

The qualified majority is set at 54 votes, thus allowing there to be a blocking minority of 23. This gives rise to negotiations and shifting alliances. Member countries have to be responsive to each other's needs, as well as the domestic lobbies.

- *Increased power for the European Parliament.* The SEA created the so-called 'co-operation procedure', for Single Market legislation which in essence gave the Parliament more bargaining power vis-a-vis the Commission and the Council of Ministers than the previous 'consultation procedure', which remains for proposals based on other treaties. (See Figure 2.1.)

The co-operation procedure, in simplified terms, has the following stages:

1. The Commission (consulting national civil servants, pressure groups, etc.) draws up a 'proposal' which it puts to the Council.
2. COREPER considers the proposal, and if agreement between member states at this stage is possible, returns it to the Council as an 'A', agreed-point. 'B' points are those which require further negotiation.
3. The Council passes the Commission's proposals to the Parliament for an 'opinion' (and, in economic and social matters, to the Economic and Social Committee, an advisory body of 189 members, 24 from the UK, consisting of representatives of employers, unions and consumers).

4. The Parliament delegates this proposal to a committee, which reports back, possibly with suggested amendments. Parliament, in a 'First Reading' then decides to accept, reject or amend the proposal. The Commission has a non-voting presence in Parliament and indicates before the vote which amendments it can accept.

5. After First Reading the (probably amended) proposal returns to the Commission which issues an amended version.

6. Following negotiations in COREPER, the Council adopts a 'common position' on the proposal, i.e., a deal they can live with, and the new text is then returned to the Parliament for Second Reading.

7. Parliament now has an opportunity, created by the SEA, to propose amendments to a common position before it is adopted. This power is subject to a time guillotine.

ROLE OF THE UK PARLIAMENT

The UK Parliament is regularly informed about EC developments and scrutinizes proposed legislation in advance. Ministers attending Council meetings always report to the House, orally or in writing. Every four weeks, there is a 20 minute Question Time on EC matters. The Government publishes a bi-annual progress report *Developments in the European Communities*, which is debated, and a separate debate is held on the EC Budget.

In the case of proposed legislation, copies of the proposals are sent to the UK Parliament (by the Government) at the same time as they go to the European Parliament and the Economic and Social Committee. The relevant UK government department provides an accompanying memorandum. These, together with the proposals, are considered by the Select Committee on European Legislation in the House of Commons (which meets weekly) and the Select Committee on the European Communities in the House of Lords. Both committees draw the attention of their respective Houses to those EC proposals which should be debated. The Government is supposed to make time available for such debates before the relevant Minister attends the EC Council meeting which is intended to pass the legislation. In practice, this does not always happen.

Thus, opportunities continue to exist to lobby the UK Parliament on EC matters of concern to you, but this cannot substitute for direct representations in Brussels.

3
The Civil Service –
Mandarins or
Managers?

Businessmen, dealing with the government departments which will be described in Part II, will always find themselves dealing with civil servants. Even on the relatively rare occasions when a meeting is arranged with a Minister, officials will always be present, will have organized the event and will follow it up.

Civil servants form the 'permanent government' in our system. In other countries, a cadre of senior officials will depart when the government changes; not so in Whitehall, where professional pride is taken in the ability and readiness to serve legitimate governments of any political complexion. For reasons we will discuss shortly the nature of the civil service is badly understood outside government, a small band of academics and the more sophisticated lobbyists.

In this chapter some of the features of the civil service will be described, together with a snapshot of the rapidly evolving changes to the service commonly referred to in the Whitehall village as the 'Next Steps' initiative.

GRADES AND TITLES

To an outsider, probably the most basic difficulty is understanding the nomenclature of civil service jobs. This task is made no easier by an official change in titles of senior grades which was never publicized effectively outside the service and has not, in the reality of language, replaced the old system, internally or externally.

There is not, and cannot be, any precise equivalence with job titles in business. (Of course, there are also vast differences between appointments

16

in business entitled 'manager' or even 'director'.)

Also, salary levels are not an accurate guide to comparability between public and private sector jobs. The following table, therefore, gives only the roughest of guides to civil service grades, and indeed only those of what

Figure 3.1 Civil Service grades

New grade	Old title	Salary (max) (1992)	
1	Permanent Secretary	£84,250	Constitutional responsibility at Grade (1) as accounting officers for the public expenditure of their
1A	Second Permanent Secretary	£77,500	departments. The overall management of those departments. The most senior inter-Whitehall negotiations. The
2	Deputy Secretary	£70,400	most senior support to Secretaries of State. Ambassadors for the department at (in big company terms) chairman level. Project managers for major initiatives, e.g., privatizations. Appointments at these levels approved by Prime Minister.
3	Under Secretary	£57,000	Managers of the work done at the next levels down. 'Front men' at
4	New grade (has no equivalent)	£49,790	appropriate meetings and presentations.
5	Assistant Secretary	£47,921	Where the work is done, either in policy jobs or in the management of substantial clerical and
6	Senior Principal	£43,724	administrative effort. These grades see through a Bill or the
7	Principal	£34,667	setting up of a new scheme (see the case study of eco-labelling in Part V) or manage significant parts of executive agencies, where chief executives are generally at grade 3 level.

The Secretary to the Cabinet and Head of the Home Civil Service receives £104,750.

The Permanent Secretary to the Treasury and the Head of the Diplomatic Service each receive £98,500.

business would generally recognise as graduate entry level. Many decisions affecting business will be taken by officials who will have entered service without graduate qualifications.

RECRUITMENT AND APPOINTMENT

The Northcote-Trevelyan Report of 1854 called for recruitment on the basis of open competition (rather than patronage) and appointment and promotion on the basis of merit. These principles apply today. The Civil Service Commission (established 1855) ensures that staff at middle and higher levels are selected solely on merit through open competition. Entry at graduate, GCE A level or GCSE level is made on the basis of tests and interviews in addition to qualifications. Departments are responsible for promotions up to grade 4. The Cabinet Office must approve appointments to grade 3, and the Prime Minister appointments to grades 1 and 2.

POLITICAL NEUTRALITY

Civil Servants, like any other citizens, will have political views and the inalienable right to belong to political parties and to vote in all elections. There are, however, limits to public political activities.

Three levels are distinguished:

- *Politically free*: industrial staff may indulge in any political activity, though if elected an MP or MEP they must resign from the civil service
- *Politically restricted*: grades 7 and above, plus administrative trainees (graduates in first appointment) cannot take part in national political activities and must apply for permission to take part in local political activities
- *Intermediate group*: all other civil servants may apply for permission to take part in national or local political activity, apart from being candidates as MPs or MEPs

The involvement of the Prime Minister in approving appointments at grades 1 and 2 (which dates from 1920) came under criticism during the premiership of Mrs Margaret Thatcher. Accusations were levelled that certain permanent secretary appointments had favoured candidates on the basis of political commitment rather than merit. This allegation was investigated and rejected both by the House of Commons Select Committee on the Treasury and Civil Service, and by a group convened by the Royal Institute of Public Administration. The verdict seems to have been that the then Prime Minister favoured candidates who appeared to her to have a more 'can-do' attitude than the traditional reflective posture of Whitehall mandarins, but no more.

Ministers of all political colours have found a way of supplementing 'neutral' Whitehall advice through the appointment of political or 'special' advisers. Frequently these are young men and women from a political party research department background. More occasionally, they are more substantial and experienced figures from business or academia or, a sign of the times, pressure groups. Such advisers are appointed as civil servants and paid out of public funds (though some, e.g., Lord Young in a previous incarnation, have served free of charge). Apart from ability, much depends on the chemistry between the individual concerned and both the Minister and the permanent officials. At worst, such appointments are frozen out of the departmental policy-making system and lapse into party political speech-writing assignments; at best they can provide a fruitful and creative input to the presentation of a Minister's case.

MINISTERIAL ACCOUNTABILITY

This doctrine states that ministers are responsible for their departments and take their decisions. Officials advise. Ministers, who must (by convention: there is no law) be members of one of the Houses of Parliament, are politicians and defend their policies and decisions in the adversarial context of Parliament. Officials, who are appointed on a non-political basis, explain rather than defend government policies or decisions. The application of this historic doctrine is evolving, as more and more of the work of government is devolved to executive agencies, but the basic principle which it enshrines lingers on and remains the single most important and negative influence on how Whitehall puts on a public face.

The problem which that creates is simply stated. The real expression of ministerial life, especially for those in the Cabinet, is a grossly overcrowded diary. Attending Parliament, whether on the floor of the House, at Select and Party committees or informally mixing with colleagues whose support they need, must be combined with work in the department plus preparing for and attending Cabinet and Cabinet committees. Ministers must also travel, regularly to Brussels on EC matters, and often elsewhere. On top of that are Party engagements, constituency duties, briefing journalists, and the vestiges of a family life.

Of course, a talented Minister, infused with the adrenalin of office, can master a formidable workload, but he simply does not have the time personally to consider every nuance of every case, consult every interested party and keep track of the evolution of policy in the sectors for which he has responsibility. Indeed, the very possibility of this latter accomplishment is often denied Ministers by the frequency with which they are shuffled. Between 1964 and 1991, the average tenure of Secretaries of State for Trade and Industry, Transport, Employment and Environment was less than two years. In the case of the DTI, there have been seven Ministers in eight years. (See Rose 1991.) These tenures are much shorter than in many EC countries. As Rose has pointed out, since the EC operates through councils of departmental Ministers, a UK Minister can be handicapped in his negotiations when dealing with counterparts who are in the job for twice as long, or in some countries, who have been civil servants with life-long experience in the subject.

The implication of this is plain. It is civil servants who conduct consultation exercises, work up material into succinct analyses, set out options for ministerial decision, and build up knowledge of their areas in depth. (Most officials spend all their working lives in the department they first joined.) These activities carry, *de facto*, considerable responsibilities and influence and yet officials feel inhibited in talking publicly about their work lest that be thought to infringe the principle of ministerial responsibility. Thus the opportunity, if not the need, for explaining the system of government has been suppressed. There have been, and are, exceptions. Individual Ministers have instructed their officials to be more outward looking. Individual civil servants – and, occasionally, Heads of the civil service – have espoused greater openness. Then a leaked document to a newspaper or Opposition politician has changed the atmosphere, and discretion has returned to the fore. Thus the stereotypes and caricatures are never properly dissipated, and an ever-slothful press is not forced to update its vocabulary of tea, mandarins and bowler hats.

Overall, it is now generally accepted that the doctrine of ministerial accountability for all operational matters in a department is unrealistic, and paying lip service to it leads to ministerial overload, frustrated officials and bad government. We discuss next in this chapter, the progress being made in delegating to executive agencies the operational work of departments, that is, delivering services such as car licences or social security benefits, which accounts for about 95 per cent of civil service manpower. The policy world inhabited by Ministers and officials operating in close support is the other five per cent.

But Whitehall does not easily lend itself to cut and dried categorization. There is a constant interaction between the execution of programmes and the evolution of policy. Hard evidence gained 'on the ground' during the operation of a scheme designed, say, to encourage technological innovation may reveal unforeseen or underestimated problems for companies seeking to adopt new technologies, thus stimulating a review of policies on innovation.

A CHANGING SCENE – DEPARTMENTS AND AGENCIES

The structure of Whitehall has never been static. Over the years, governments of all complexions have regularly created, merged and abolished departments. Such changes have tended to be in response to specific requirements or motivations, e.g., providing a counterbalance to the Treasury's dominance over economic policy by the creation of the Department of Economic Affairs in 1964. In recent years, however, there has emerged a systematic approach to the restructuring of Whitehall which will leave no department untouched. It is known as the 'Next Steps' initiative, after the name of a seminal report to the Prime Minister by the Efficiency Unit in 1987.

The central concept is that as much as 95 per cent of the work of the civil service comprises the delivery of services to citizens, ranging from welfare benefits to weather forecasts. Only a tiny fraction of Whitehall is engaged in giving policy advice to Ministers. Yet, in the traditional set-up, not only did policy work co-exist with executive work in a monolithic departmental structure, but the path to the most senior civil service jobs was seen to lie in the policy area. Further, since the higher reaches of policy work involves providing close support to Ministers, there emerged in the top management positions in Whitehall a breed, not of administrative generalists as sometimes depicted, but rather one of political specialists.

It has now been recognized that the tasks of improving the delivery of public services to customers, obtaining better value for taxpayers' money, and enhancing the jobs of public service employees are all better done by devolving responsibility for executive work away from centralized departments to executive agencies, each headed by a chief executive responsible to a Minister for the operational management of the function concerned.

In this approach, familiar in business but something of a revolution to the civil service, the chief executive is given resources and targets by his

Minister, appropriate control systems are installed, and he gets on with running the organization as he sees fit, taking day-to-day managerial decisions in the light of what is best for the achievement of his targets, and not according to some universal civil service rule book. Each agency will be different, because the tasks differ so greatly.

It will be appreciated that converting this concept into reality is a substantial and difficult task. Not only does the civil service have the inbuilt inertia of any organization of its size and history, but the changes have to be accomplished while demonstrably preserving both control over public expenditure and accountability to Parliament. Given this background, the achievements of the Next Steps project are impressive. The original report advocating the new approach was delivered to the Prime Minister in Spring 1987. Mrs Thatcher announced the Government's acceptance of the recommendations in February 1988. By the end of July 1988, 29 candidates for agency status had been identified, with a further 37 under consideration. On 1 August 1988, the first agency – the Vehicle Inspectorate of the Department of Transport – was launched. As of October 1991, there were 56 agencies employing 200,000 people – approaching 40 per cent of all civil servants.

There has been considerable progress in installing – and meeting – performance targets. In 1991, of the agencies with a full year's record to show, and leaving aside the target they are all set to stay within their budgets, the results were:

- 53 quality of service targets set; 37 met or bettered
- 26 financial performance targets set; 20 met or bettered
- 38 efficiency targets met or bettered

Open competition has been used to recruit the chief executives. Two thirds have come from the civil service and one third from elsewhere. Eleven per cent are women, nearly twice the percentage in the equivalent ranks of the civil service as a whole.

The names of the agencies established and activities announced by departments to be under consideration as of October 1991 are set out in Appendix C.

Almost all the agencies do or will interact with business. The implications for business are that problems relating to services provided should be fewer, and soluble more quickly, arising out of a more managerial, devolved and businesslike approach within the agencies. Further, it was suggested in the original Efficiency Unit report that in future, civil servants heading for senior positions should have had successful experience in both executive and policy work. To the extent that this happens, policy advice to Ministers should increasingly reflect practical managerial experience. Time will tell.

DEPARTMENTAL PROFILES

The departmental profiles which follow in Part II are therefore snapshots taken during a period of considerable structural change in Whitehall. In addition to structure, the particular policies pursued in individual departments will change, sometimes very rapidly, as Ministers change, as the world changes, and when there is a change of government. Although any description of what a department does will thus inevitably reflect the prevailing policy orientation, there is a substantial degree of continuity in the areas of work, if not in the organizational structures or detailed policies.

To give a full description of the work of every department would be both excessively lengthy and tedious to read, since most businesses are affected by only a few departments. The principle adopted, therefore, is to group the departments, in declining length of description, as follows:

The primary group
Departments whose activities are likely to impinge on most businesses:
- Department of Trade and Industry (DTI)
- Department of Employment (DE)
- Department of the Environment (DoE)
- Department of Transport (DTp)
- HM Treasury (including Inland Revenue, HM Customs)
- Office of Fair Trading (OFT) and the Monopolies and Mergers Commission (MMC); and the utility Regulators

Major sectoral departments
Departments which have a very significant impact on discrete but important individual sectors of the economy:
- Ministry of Defence, Procurement Executive (MoD/PE)
- Ministry of Agriculture, Fisheries and Food (MAFF)
- Department of Energy (DEn)

Minor sectoral departments
Departments which have an impact on a more restricted number of businesses, or a restricted impact on business generally:
- Department of Health (DoH)

- Overseas Development Administration (ODA)
- Foreign and Commonwealth Office (FCO)
- The National Economic Development Office (NEDO)

Although many government departments deal with the UK as a whole, others do not; and indeed, within some departments like MAFF, Employment or Education and Science, the writ runs differently for different programmes, as the chart illustrates. This is mainly due to the administrative autonomy granted to Scotland, Wales and Northern Ireland, for historical, cultural and political reasons.

Figure 3.2 Geographical responsibility of some government departments

UK	England, Scotland and Wales	England and Wales	England
HM Customs	DE (most)	Home Office	DES
MoD	DSS (Department of	(other)	(Education)
DEn	Social Security)		DE
FCO	DTI (ex regional		(Careers)
MAFF (Food)	assistance)		DoE
Home Office	DTp (ex motorways)		DoH
(Broadcasting)	DES (Department of		DTp
HM Treasury	Education and Science)		(Motorways)
Inland Revenue	(Universities)		MAFF
DES (Department	OFFER		(Other)
of Education and			DTI
Science)			(regional
OFGAS			assistance)
OFTEL			
ODA			

What business needs to know is that, with some variations, the Scottish, Welsh and Northern Ireland Offices have responsibilities for: agriculture and fisheries; town and country planning; environmental protection; water and sewerage; selective financial assistance and regional development grants to industry; urban renewal; training and industrial development; encouragement of exports and of inward investment; tourism; and roads and public transport. Local businesses, concerned about matters falling under those headings, should therefore contact those Offices in the first instance.

It should be noted, local sensitivities notwithstanding, that in economic and industrial matters, UK policies generally prevail. The regional offices in effect administer national DTI programmes like the various aspects of the Enterprise Initiative. When devolution has extended to the transfer, from the Department of Employment to the Scottish Office, of budgetary responsibility for training and enterprise programmes, this has been in the context of a ministerial agreement that, in Scotland, national programmes will be delivered to national standards.

For a broad understanding of the processes of government as they affect business, therefore, the following description of Whitehall departments will assume a general impact on UK business as a whole.

As this book went to press, the General Election of 9 April 1992 returned a Conservative Government, and shortly thereafter a number of changes to the machinery of government started to be announced. Of principal interest to business, the Department of Energy is disbanded, with most of its functions going to the DTI, except the Energy Efficiency Office, which goes to the Department of the Environment. Responsibility for the financial services industry moves from DTI to the Treasury. Responsibility for small businesses moves from the Department of Employment to DTI. The new Department of National Heritage takes responsibility for broadcasting from the Home Office and for tourism from the Department of Employment. DTI takes over aspects of urban regeneration from the Department of the Environment.

The fine detail of Departmental re-organization consequent upon these changes of responsibility will obviously take time to be worked out, but the overall architecture of Whitehall as it pertains to most businesses is substantially unchanged.

4
Whitehall,
Westminster and
Beyond

Parliament is the focus of national political life, and the arrival of television cameras in the Chamber has consolidated this position. Ministers are recruited solely from Parliament and are answerable to it. This accountability is taken seriously. Ministerial reputations can be irretrievably damaged by a poor performance at the Despatch Box. A skilful speech by a backbencher, noted by the whips, is often the stepping stone to a junior ministerial job. Much work is done in Whitehall preparing for debates, answering questions or appearing before select committees, in addition, of course, to that involved when legislation is being prepared.

Business people therefore need to know at what point issues of concern to them will enter the Parliamentary domain, in what form, and how they can be addressed. Part III analyses the relevant structures and procedures within Parliament and discusses how best to capture the attention of MPs, who are the target of countless other approaches.

The activities of Parliament and of Westminster politicians are well-reported by the media. As has been discussed, Whitehall is inadequately covered. But even a full reporting of both Westminster and Whitehall mechanics would be an insufficient guide to the way in which policies are formed and decisions are taken. Other groups are intimately involved in the process. Figure 4.1 illustrates, in outline, some of the complexity which has to be addressed if a thorough and systematic approach to business representation is to be undertaken.

The influence of some organizations such as consumers, environmentalists and the business lobby is so great that they are discussed separately in Part IV.

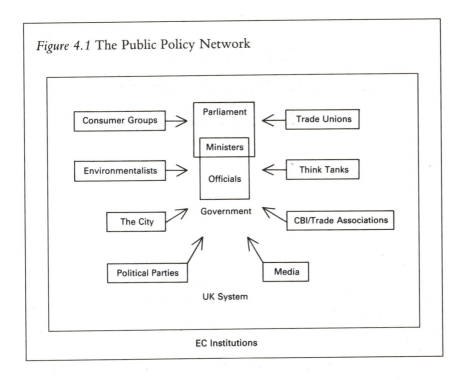

Figure 4.1 The Public Policy Network

For the businessman who wishes to understand our system of government and to represent his concerns within it, perhaps the single most important point to grasp is that the various interest and other groups depicted in the diagram do not exist in splendid isolation. They interact. The Confederation of British Industry (CBI) consults its members (including trade associations) about various issues and makes representations direct to the appropriate government departments. But it also lobbies Members of Parliament and briefs the media.

On financial matters, financial journalists – whose stories are read by Ministers and officials – regularly report the comments of City analysts, not only on company performance but on the impact of government policies on companies. Companies who have the knowledge and ability will have briefed the relevant analysts, and their views will stand a good chance of being reported.

Officials will ensure that they are aware of the position of the relevant pressure groups or interest groups on the issues being considered by their Ministers; and will indeed consult them formally and regularly. This not only reflects the sheer political importance of interest groups (there are more members of environmental organizations than of political parties) but also their expertise and grass roots contacts. Single issue pressure groups, e.g., the Child Poverty Action Group, or Shelter, will over time accumulate an expertise on aspects of their particular policy issues which is superior to that of the relevant government departments. When a major pressure group like Consumers' Association campaigns on car prices or producer liability, Ministers and officials will take notice, because they will know that an organization, well supported by ordinary citizens/voters, has researched a subject (albeit not always perfectly) and is well versed in gaining the attention of the media.

Think tanks, such as the Centre for Policy Studies (CPS), on the right, or the Centre for Public Policy Research, on the left, generally play a minor part in policy formation, though they can have their moments, as did the CPS during the Thatcher years, with special relevance to privatization. As with trade associations, insufficient resources have been devoted in the UK to enable properly funded and staffed independent institutions to emerge and play the sort of leading role associated with, say the Brookings Institute in Washington. Nevertheless, organizations such as the Centre for Policy Studies, the Institute for Economic Affairs and the Royal Institute for International Affairs provide a mixture of original research and a networking capability which has a modest but discernible impact on the Whitehall village.

The City also undertakes research, networking and lobbying. The Bank of England, the Stock Exchange, Lloyds, the clearing and merchant banks, major fund managers and broking houses, etc., all have their fragmented communications capabilities. Much store is set on personal contacts and private discussions and it is difficult to make an accurate assessment of their overall effectiveness.

Obviously, the trade unions, as opinion-formers, have languished during the Thatcher years, but they remain connected to Whitehall and Brussels through ACAS (The Advisory, Conciliation and Arbitration Service), NEDO, ECOSOC (The Economic and Social Committee of the EC) etc., and of course maintain their position within the Labour Party and other institutions of the left. Similarly, the research departments of the political parties wax and wane but are permanent features of the structure. Apart from the content of their research, they are also important as a recruitment source both of prospective parliamentary candidates and, more relevant to the present discussion, of special advisers to Ministers, with an office in Whitehall departments and the technical status of civil servants.

The role of the media is vitally important in enabling the various groupings, as well as Ministers and (usually anonymous) officials to be seen to be participating in the policy-making process. Interest groups will have direct, bilateral conversations with government departments, but they will also ensure that the press are properly briefed, both to put pressure on Ministers and demonstrate to their membership that they are active. Finally, there is, of course, the increasingly important role of EC institutions in the policy-making process, which was covered in broad outline in Chapter 2.

To be, and to be seen to be, serious lobbyists of government, business needs to grapple with the complex reality of the inputs made to government. Clearly, there will be many different constellations of groupings surrounding the decision-makers, depending on the subject. A member of the nuclear industry will be concerned about the anti-nuclear stance of a future Labour Government and will therefore wish to explore the trade union position, and cultivate energy correspondents in the press. A supermarket chain will be concerned more with consumer organizations and the Office of Fair Trading's interest in pricing policies, and so on.

Some business issues can be dealt with, perfectly satisfactorily, by properly structured bilateral conversations with Whitehall officials. Part V deals with the rules of engagement with civil servants. But often there will be a need to participate in the wider network bearing upon the particular issue of concern. Here the businessman needs to identify who is relevant, and when and how to intervene. In other words, a campaign of sorts may need to be mounted. Part V also sets out the parameters for that activity.

Part II

A Businessman's Map of Whitehall

Departmental Profiles

5
Department of
Trade and Industry

OBJECTIVES

The DTI is of signal importance to British business not only because of its directly relevant domestic responsibilities but also because, within Whitehall, it is the lead department on the European Community proposals for a single market by end-1992. Under successive Secretaries of State in Conservative Governments since 1979, the Department has progressively, if unsteadily, disengaged itself from the interventionist role it had under previous administrations. In its latest guise, it provides a wide range of services to business, publishes a vast amount of information, and finances a variety of schemes to improve business performance. It is therefore vital for business to understand its attitude and programme of activities.

The fact that there have been eight Secretaries of State between 1979 and 1991 has inevitably created some jerkiness in the department's voyage from being effective owner and proactive sponsor of large tracts of British industry to a position best described by the Statement of Departmental Objectives published in April 1991:

The aim of the Department of Trade and Industry is to foster a market environment which results in satisfied customers and prosperous producers. To this end the DTI works to ensure that markets at home and abroad are open, fair and competitive; to see that UK business is best placed to take full advantage of market opportunities; and to champion all those involved in wealth creation.

The DTI will:

• Work for trade liberalization worldwide, and the completion of the

Single European Market
- Promote exports of UK goods and services
- Stimulate innovation in industry by encouraging research, the transfer of technologies, the spread of technical skills and closer links between business and the science base
- Improve the provision of information to business about new methods, opportunities and management skills
- Encourage competition by tackling restrictive practices, cartels and monopolies, and by extending privatization and contracting out
- Foster the integrity of markets so that customers, creditors and investors benefit from a well-targeted system of protection and a light but effective regulatory framework allowing informed choices to be made
- Encourage a positive attitude towards wealth creation
- Reduce burdens on business by simplifying regulation and scrutinizing the compliance costs which regulation brings
- Listen to the concerns of business and consumers and ensure that these are taken into account in the development of government policies
- Ensure that policies respond to the needs of different regions and areas with special difficulties.

In order to achieve these objectives the DTI is committed to managing and developing the people who work within it, to enable them to provide a professional, high quality, accessible and responsive service to business and the community.

STRUCTURE

These objectives are pursued within a structure set out in Figure 5.1.

Of the DTI's staff of just under 12,000, about half work in the ten executive agencies. Also, over half of the Department's staff are based outside London, either working in one of the agencies or in the department's network of regional offices in England. (See Appendix D.)

It will be seen that, within the central structure of the Department, the British Overseas Trade Board retains its own identity, reflecting the previous separate departmental and ministerial existence of 'Trade', as distinct from 'Industry'. The two Departments were first brought together by Edward Heath in 1970, separated by Harold Wilson in 1974, and reunited by Margaret Thatcher in 1983. The Industry side of the Department

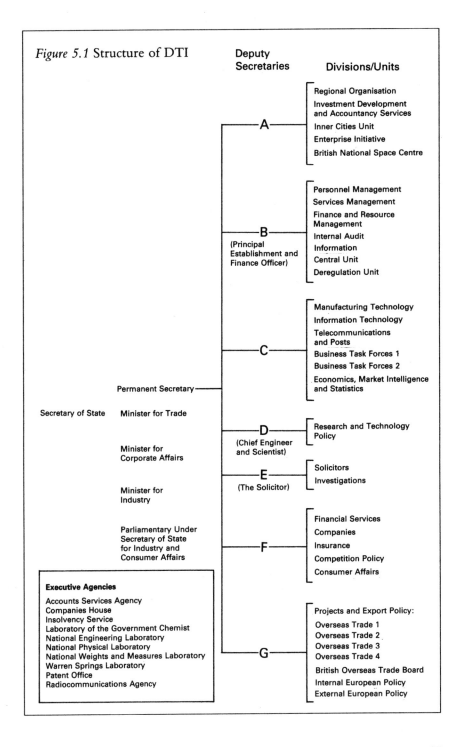

Figure 5.1 Structure of DTI

was organised in substantially the traditional manner – vertical divisions sponsoring sectors of industry – until 1987, when Lord Young was appointed Secretary of State. He conducted a fundamental review of the Department's mission and virtually renamed it 'the Department for Enterprise' in 1988.

The concept was to re-orientate the Department's work away from industrial sectors and towards a focus on markets – making them more competitive by attacking restrictive practices and monopolies; making them more efficient by improving the flow of information to business; making them larger by privatization; and making them fairer by improving consumer and investor protection. The term 'sponsor' was dropped from the Department's vocabulary and, for example, the Vehicles Division, previously the 'sponsor' of the vehicles and components industries, was renamed Vehicles Markets Division, to remove any interpretation that its purpose was to reflect a particular producer interest.

Lord Young's successors, Nicholas Ridley and Peter Lilley, continued that approach. A review of the Department's structure in 1989/90 led to the virtual abolition of all the vertically organized Markets Divisions dealing with specific market sectors and their replacement by horizontal units, e.g., 'manufacturing technology', responsible for delivering DTI services of a particular kind to many types of businesses. Reality, of course, intervenes to frustrate the purity of all organizational principles. There is a unique cluster of issues surrounding the vehicles, aerospace and shipbuilding industries, where the Government has to play a significant role, e.g., in negotiating local content criteria for Japanese car manufacturers with the EC. This has been found to justify a dedicated structure to deal with those sectors, at any rate for so long as the issues remain live. That conundrum was elegantly resolved by locating responsibility for those industries in units called 'Business Task Forces', a term redolent of impermanence.

WHAT DOES THE DTI DO?

Leaving aside the tasks of the executive agencies, which are largely self-explanatory, the mainstream work of the Department falls under the following broad heads, which are those the Department uses in reporting its expenditure plans and performance to Parliament. The financial figures quoted, which provide some perspective on the resources devoted to the policies, are the estimated out-turns of public expenditure on these programmes in 1990/91. They exclude the central running cost of the Department (£268m).

Regional and general industrial support (£321m)

- Through Regional Selective Assistance and Regional Enterprise Grants, funds for investment projects are available in the Assisted Areas
- Inner Cities: DTI operates some 16 Inner City Task Forces in the most deprived urban areas, with the purpose of creating employment and developing enterprise
- Consultancy initiatives: Small and medium sized firms are given subsidized access to external consultants for short term advice on design, marketing, quality, manufacturing systems, business planning, financial and information systems

Support for industry (£424m)

These programmes fall into two main categories: those applying to industry in general and those which bear upon particular industries. Under the former heading are innovation; education and training; design and management; and inward investment.

Innovation

DTI encourages innovation through support for collaborative projects, technology transfer and measures for small firms.

Programmes promoting collaboration are as follows:

- *LINK*, which encourages firms to work jointly with universities and other research organizations on pre-competitive research
- *EUREKA*, which provides a framework for collaboration between European firms using advanced technology
- *Advanced Technology Programme*, which encourages UK companies to collaborate in pre-competitive research in new technology
- General industrial collaboration projects, in particular DTI support for industry-led projects undertaken through research and technology organizations

Technology transfer programmes are accomplished mainly via the network of 13 regional technology centres and are aimed particularly at small and medium sized enterprises (SMEs).

Education and Training
Although a substantial part of DTI's education and training work, mainly related to schools, was transferred to the Department of Employment in early 1991, the Department still encourages links between business and education, for example, through the *Teaching Company Scheme*, whereby young graduates carry out key projects in companies under the joint supervision of academics and company staff.

Design and Management
The DTI uses the Design Council to assist British manufacturing companies in developing better products through design. Through the *Managing into the 90s* programme, best management practice is encouraged, especially in the areas of quality, purchasing, design and production management – again aimed mainly at SMEs.

Inward investment
There are three elements concerned with the promotion of inward investment:

- The DTI's Invest in Britain Bureau, which represents the UK as a whole
- The five Regional Development Organizations (RDOs) part-funded by DTI. Each represents an area of England and promotes it to potential investors
- The DTI's English Unit. This promotes England overseas as a location for inward investment, working with RDOs and DTI Regional Offices in non-RDO regions

Support for aerospace shipbuilding and steel (£159m)
Special measures are in force to provide launch aid for civil aerospace projects (recouped from levies on subsequent sales); to finance research on airframe technology, avionics and propulsion systems; to allow UK shipowners to order ships in the UK on terms competitive with the export credit terms of other shipbuilding nations; and to assist steel industry restructuring by cushioning the effect on steelworkers made redundant.

International trade (£54m)
The two main elements are export promotion and the Single Market campaign. The Department provides a wide range of services and schemes to support UK exporters. In financial terms, the largest single element is

assistance to enable firms to take part in overseas trade fairs.

The Single Market campaign, which has cost £22m in the three years since its inception in March 1988, is intended to inform British firms about the changes likely to arise from the EC's 1992 programme, and to help them prepare for those changes. Following an initial attention-raising advertising campaign, the emphasis has been on providing a comprehensive information service for companies and trade associations.

Consumer and investor protection (£107m)
Expenditure in this area covers:

- The costs of the Monopolies and Mergers Commission
- Grants to consumer organizations
- The Financial Reporting Council, set up in 1990 to improve the quality of accounting standards and oversee their application
- Other investor protection costs, including the costs of Companies Act and Financial Services Act investigations

6
Department of Employment

The Department of Employment is now referred to in Whitehall as the Employment Department Group, and consists of four main elements:

- The Employment Department Headquarters
- The Employment Service (an executive agency)
- The Health and Safety Commission (HSC) and its operational arm, the Health and Safety Executive (HSE)
- The Advisory, Conciliation and Arbitration Service (ACAS)

In recent years, the thrust of the Department's activity has moved away from the reform of trade union and industrial relations legislation towards the uprating of the national skill and enterprise base. Not only is this subject of direct and vital concern to business, employers are being involved to an unprecedented extent, in planning and delivering the programmes necessary to meet that objective, in the process assuming responsibility for spending around £3 billion of public funds.

AIMS AND OBJECTIVES

Aim
To support economic growth by promoting a competitive, efficient and flexible labour market.

Objectives
To help secure a skilled and productive workforce:

- To get employers to take effective action to ensure that people at all levels have the skills required to meet the needs of industry and commerce
- To get individuals to take more responsibility for their own development
- To help ensure that the education system gives young people a proper foundation for work
- To promote more effective systems and methods in training

To promote enterprise and the generation of new jobs:

- To encourage arrangements that enable pay to respond flexibly to labour market conditions and to performance
- To encourage self-employment and the development of small firms
- To develop the contribution the tourism industry makes to economic and employment growth

To help people get jobs, particularly those who are unemployed:

- To provide particular help to people who are long-term unemployed, who have disabilities or other disadvantages and those living in inner cities to find and retain jobs
- To make sure that unemployed people in receipt of benefits are available for and actively seeking work; and to discourage benefit fraud
- To ensure accurate and prompt payment of benefits to people who remain unemployed

To promote a fair and safe environment for work:

- To protect people at work and the public from industrial risks
- To ensure equality of opportunity in the labour market
- To ensure that the essential employment rights of individuals are safeguarded
- To maintain a fair balance under the law between management, organized labour and individuals and to facilitate good industrial relations
- To encourage people to be involved in and committed to the success of their enterprise

In pursuing this aim and these objectives the Department will:

- Ensure that international policies, particularly those of the European Community, take full account of UK labour market policies and programmes
- Use its resources in a cost effective way
- Promote the development of appropriate skills and competence among its own staff

Figure 6.1 shows the structure of the Employment Department Group

EMPLOYMENT DEPARTMENT HEADQUARTERS

The Employment Department headquarters employs around 12,000 staff organised into three directorates covering separate areas of responsibility. Directorates are further split into divisions and branches. Main locations are in London, Runcorn and Sheffield.

Training, Enterprise and Education Directorate (TEED)

TEED covers the work formerly done by the Training Agency and is mainly based in Sheffield. It is responsible for training, enterprise and education policy; work on training standards and systems and direct delivery of some programmes such as the Small Firms Loan Guarantee Scheme.

The Government White Paper *Employment for the 1990s* (1988) set out major changes at national, industry and local level to provide a modern framework for training. The key element of this new approach was the setting up of a network of 82 locally-based employer-led bodies, known as Training and Enterprise Councils (TECs), throughout England and Wales. Similar bodies are being set up in Scotland. Through its regional offices, TEED negotiates and monitors contracts with TECs for the local provision of government-funded training and enterprise programmes (see below).

Areas of responsibility include:

- Adult training
- Youth training
- Training credits
- Career development loans
- Education/business partnerships
- Work-related further education
- Enterprise in higher education
- Technical Vocational Education Initiative

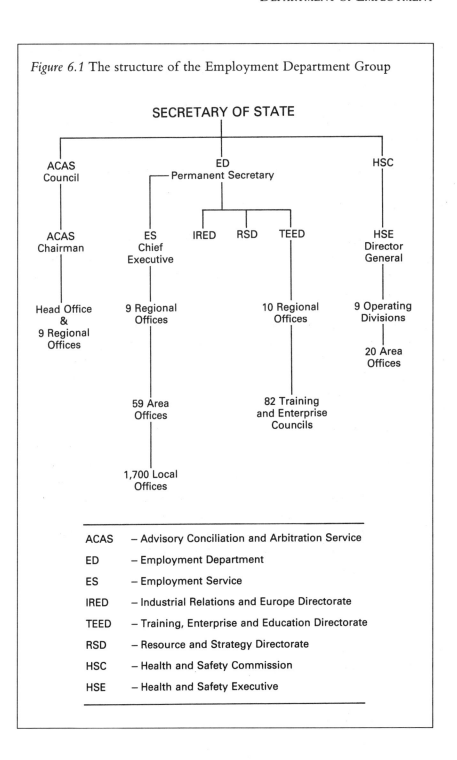

Figure 6.1 The structure of the Employment Department Group

ACAS	– Advisory Conciliation and Arbitration Service
ED	– Employment Department
ES	– Employment Service
IRED	– Industrial Relations and Europe Directorate
TEED	– Training, Enterprise and Education Directorate
RSD	– Resource and Strategy Directorate
HSC	– Health and Safety Commission
HSE	– Health and Safety Executive

- Enterprise Allowance Scheme
- Loan Guarantee Scheme
- Support for self-employed small firms
- Business communications
- Careers service
- Training quality
- Training standards
- Industry training organizations
- Learning systems
- Training access

The Industrial Relations and Europe Directorate (IRED)

IRED, based mainly in London, is responsible for the promotion of a competitive and efficient labour market by improving industrial relations, removing barriers to employment growth and safeguarding the employment rights of individuals. The Directorate is also responsible for ensuring that international policies, particularly those of the European Community, take full account of UK employment policies and practices.

Areas of responsibility include:

- Industrial relations
- Pay
- Equal opportunities
- Employee rights/employee involvement
- Relations with the European Community
- Relations with international organizations (the ILO, the OECD, the Council of Europe) and with overseas governments
- Statistics
- Tourism
- Liaison with Health and Safety Executive
- Employment agency leasing
- Work permit scheme
- Wages councils

Resources and Strategy Directorate (RSD)

RSD provides corporate services (finance, staff development and business services) and economics, research and evaluation support to all staff in the Employment Department Headquarters. It is mainly based in Runcorn. It also has a new strategy unit, other employment and policy briefing work (including monitoring the performance of the Employment Service Agency

under the framework agreement), and information policy.
Areas of responsibility include:

- Personnel management and staff development
- Information systems and technical services
- Economic briefing and labour market analysis
- Employment policy briefing
- Research and evaluation
- Information (publications, press office, marketing/publicity)

THE EMPLOYMENT SERVICE

The Employment Service was established as an executive agency within the Employment Department Group in April 1990. It has about 36,000 staff and a network of about 1,700 local offices throughout Great Britain and is responsible for providing services and administering programmes to help people get jobs.
Its main objectives are to:

- Provide unemployed people, particularly those who have been unemployed for longer than six months and those in the inner cities, with job opportunities and help in job search skills, or opportunities to become self-employed or to find appropriate training
- Provide particular assistance to people with a disability to take advantage of work and training opportunities; and to help and encourage employers to make such opportunities available
- Pay benefit promptly, accurately and courteously
- Encourage unemployed claimants to seek work actively; and to check that they are entitled to unemployment benefit, national insurance credits or, as an unemployed person, to income support, in accordance with social security legislation
- Discourage benefit fraud by identifying, investigating and where appropriate prosecuting those suspected of, or colluding in, obtaining benefit by deception

THE HEALTH AND SAFETY COMMISSION AND EXECUTIVE

The HSC and HSE were created by The Health and Safety at Work Act 1974.

The Commission is appointed by the Secretary of State for Employment and consists of a chairman and nine members representing employers, trade unions, local authorities, and the public interest. It is responsible to a number of secretaries of state for the administration of various aspects of the 1974 Act and of related legislation, while for administrative and financial purposes forming part of the Employment Department Group and exercising a considerable independence of government in its day-to-day functions though subject to ministerial direction.

The Commission's main operational arm is the Health and Safety Executive. Their joint aims are to protect the health, safety and welfare of employees, and to safeguard others, principally the public, who may be exposed to risks from industrial activity.

The Executive has a staff of about 3,750 people of which around half are highly technically qualified and appointed either as inspectors, scientists or technological and medical specialists.

It is statutorily distinct from the Commission and apart from advising the Commission and preparing regulations, or other standards, and consulting on its behalf, it has the special function of enforcing the 1974 Act and related legislation in factories, mines, nuclear establishments, farms, on the railways and in other industrial establishments; it cannot be directed by the Commission in any particular case and it acts also as a licensing authority, e.g., in connection with nuclear sites. In 1990 it assumed full responsibility for nuclear safety research and in 1991 for offshore oil safety, both from the Department of Energy. In 1990 it also took over the functions of the Railway Inspectorate from the Department of Transport.

THE ADVISORY CONCILIATION AND ARBITRATION SERVICE

The Advisory Conciliation and Arbitration Service (ACAS) was set up as an independent body in 1974 and has about 600 staff. The Employment Protection Act 1975 established the Service as a statutory body, with the general duty of improving industrial relations.

The Service:

- Offers conciliation and arbitration in industrial disputes
- Is responsible for attempting conciliation in complaints of infringement of individual employee rights

- Gives advice on all aspects of industrial relations and employment policies to both sides of industry
- Promotes through its Work Research Unit the improvement of work structures and the quality of working life

TRAINING AND ENTERPRISE COUNCILS (TECs)

The full network of 82 TECs in England and Wales was put into operation during 1991, two years ahead of schedule. Over 1,200 business leaders at local level are involved as well as some 5,000 staff. (In Scotland, two new bodies have been created – Scottish Enterprise and Highlands and Islands Enterprise – with responsibility for training and enterprise programmes amongst other things. They will work through a network of 22 local enterprise companies. A framework has been agreed between the Secretaries of State for Employment and Scotland for the delivery of national programmes to national standards.)

Although the TECs will start on the basis of delivering the training and enterprise programmes previously run by the Employment Department, YTS, Employment Training, etc., they have a remit to develop these and, in addition, to encourage improvements in the quality and quantity of local firms' in-house training.

Each TEC has a Local Initiative Fund – which it can increase by raising money locally – to enable it to produce innovative solutions to local training and enterprise requirements.

The boards of TECs are composed of two-thirds private sector employers, at chief executive level, and one-third from education, economic development, unions, voluntary organizations and the public sector.

Each TEC is an independent legal entity which contracts with the Employment Department to deliver certain quantified targets such as job placement rates and numbers of qualifications attained. TECs which exceed their targets will be given a bonus which will be added to their Local Initiative Fund.

7
Department of the Environment

The Department has responsibility for environmental protection and water, countryside and wildlife, built heritage, land use planning, inner city housing, new towns, the construction industry and local government.

It has two executive agencies, the Building Research Establishment and the Queen Elizabeth II Conference Centre, and three other parts of the Department, including Her Majesty's Inspectorate of Pollution. In 1990 the former Property Services Agency was split into PSA Services, which provides on a competitive basis a range of property-related services, mainly to government departments; and Property Holdings, a directorate general of the Department, which is responsible for managing the government's office buildings and will act as the vendor in the privatization of PSA Services and the Crown Suppliers.

The Department is also responsible for 29 executive sponsored bodies, including the Audit Commission, the Housing Corporation, the National Rivers Authority and 10 urban development corporations, including that for London Docklands. Of its total expenditure of £29 bn, no less than £25 bn is accounted for by its financial support of English local authorities.

The organisation structure at the top of the Department is shown in Figure 7.1, and the distribution of the Department's 6,200 staff by work areas in Figure 7.2.

Although there are business implications in almost all the Department's activities, e.g., the care of historic buildings makes an important contribution to the tourist industry, it is clear that the main impact of the Department on business will be felt in the areas of:

- Environmental protection and pollution control

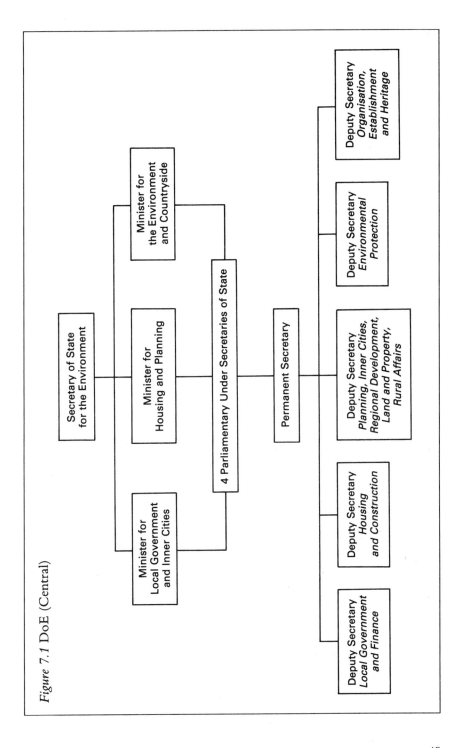

Figure 7.1 DoE (Central)

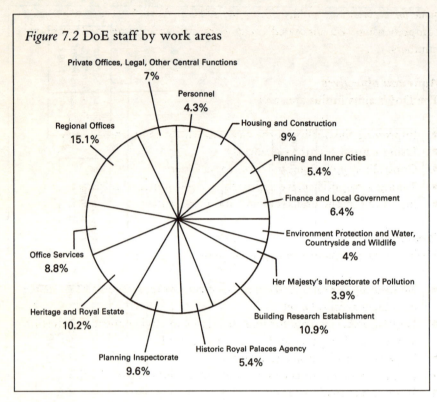

Figure 7.2 DoE staff by work areas

- The construction industry
- Inner cities

ENVIRONMENTAL PROTECTION AND POLLUTION CONTROL

A major landmark in the evolution of environmental policy and of the importance attributed to it across all Whitehall departments, was the publication of the Environment White Paper *This Common Inheritance* (CM 1200, September 1990). This provided a comprehensive coverage of all aspects of the environment, with a full statement of government activities and a commitment to use annual departmental reports to describe follow-up action. Thus, all government departments, not just DoE, report each year on their progress in pursuing various environmental concerns. The White Paper included a government commitment to issue a guide which would enable business to get in touch with environmental contacts in government departments. The first issue of this *Environmental Contacts, a guide for business* was published by the DTI in April 1991 and provides a comprehensive and annotated list of contacts, with names and telephone numbers.

Aims and objectives
The DoE's aims in this area are:

- Improving the quality of the environment in town and country
- Using natural resources prudently
- Controlling pollution of air, land and water
- Taking a comprehensive approach to environmental impacts
- Increasing public understanding and involvement

Programme
The principal means of meeting these aims are:

- Monitoring, research and appraisal of environmental impacts to enable clear standards to be set
- Legislation to regulate for high standards in environmental protection and appropriate penalties for failure to comply
- Inspectorates to enforce standards
- Financial support to encourage individual and corporate action
- Work in international fora
- Publicity and information to increase public awareness

Details of all these activities are to be found in the Departmental report and other publications. The primary impact on business will arise from the implementation of legislation to protect the environment. The foundation is the Environmental Protection Act 1990, which introduced a system of integrated pollution control (IPC); new arrangements for better waste disposal and recycling; tough penalties for noise and other pollution offences; and a new regime to prevent littering. Under the IPC the major sources of industrial pollution of air, land and water are regulated by Her Majesty's Inspectorate of Pollution (HMIP). Local authorities have responsibilities for controlling air pollution from some less complex processes.

All individual processes subject to IPC under HMIP will be required to apply 'Best Available Techniques Not Entailing Excessive Costs' to limit emissions of pollutants. Authorizations will be based on the best practical environmental option to minimize the total impact, with the object of minimizing the more serious pollutants at source and rendering all releases harmless. The new system is being phased in, with full implementation by April 1996. A detailed implementation programme was published in November 1990. HMIP's staffing is being increased to support its enhanced role, including the monitoring and inspection of industry. Its cost of operating IPC will be met from the charges to operators for authorizations. HMIP is consulting industry on the implementation of IPC and aims to issue guidance notes at least six months before each stage of the process is implemented between 1991 and 1996.

The Construction Industry

Aims and objectives

- To stimulate enterprise by promoting an understanding within the industry of market opportunities
- To encourage the industry to prepare fully for the advent of the Single European Market and to ensure that the interests of the UK construction industry are taken into account
- To influence the development of EC legislation and implement it as appropriate
- To remove practices and reform institutions which act as a bar to competition within the construction industry
- To achieve the least burdensome regulatory framework for the construction industry which is consistent with the public interest
- To maintain and develop the system of building control and promote the development of effective standards in relation to health and safety and environmental issues.

Means of delivery

DoE Ministers and officials liaise closely with professional institutions, trade associations and individual companies in the construction industry. In addition, the Department:

- Provides financial support for, and is involved in, market assessments and the promotion of standards
- Participates in ministerially-led trade missions abroad to promote UK construction knowledge
- Promotes awareness of the Single Market through *Euronews Construction* and the European Consultative Group

- Serves on the EC Standing Committee for Construction
- Drafts building regulations to ensure that construction work meets minimum standards relating to health and safety and environmental considerations, including energy efficiency and access for disabled people
- Encourages the efficient and effective operation of the building control system
- Sponsors research for the maintenance and development of building regulations and standards for construction performance
- Sponsors the British Board of Agrément, a testing and assessment organization for building and construction products

Implementation – Construction markets and technology

There are well over 100 UK trade and professional organizations representing the interests of the construction industry. Market information is disseminated to the industry through ministerial and official contact with these organizations at meetings and industry-organized events.

Euronews Construction, a newsletter edited by the Department is the principal vehicle for disseminating information about European Community legislation and related developments affecting the UK construction industry.

The European Consultative Group (ECG), chaired by the Department, provides a forum for the exchange of information and views on current EC legislation. The Group has over 40 members representing government departments and trade and professional organizations within the UK construction industry.

The Department encourages the industry to undertake collaborative European market assessments of specific sectors of the construction industry. The object is to promote awareness of market opportunities in Europe and identify potential barriers to trade which require action in the context of the Single Market programme.

Active two-way communication with representatives of industry (producers, specifiers, testing bodies, etc.), formally through two advisory committees as well as informally on an ad hoc basis, keeps the UK industry informed of developments on product standards, etc., and provides briefings for the DoE delegates to the EC Standing Committee. These delegates contribute to negotiations on Europe and to decisions affecting the UK.

DoE is the lead department for the UK in preparing regulations to implement the EC Construction Products Directive, which aims to open up free trade in construction products across the Community. Input to standards-making bodies in the UK and Europe, and close links with the British Board of Agrément also enable policy on product standards, etc., to be developed and implemented in an informed manner, and provide for interested parties in industry to be consulted and kept informed on developments. Procedures for attestation of conformity of products, and in particular designation of a number of approved European technical approval bodies, certification bodies, laboratories and test houses, are being developed.

The Department provides funding for the development of codes of practice that are in the public interest and, in particular, to represent UK interests. The Department participates in the EC working groups and in the work of CEN (the European Standards-making organisation).

INNER CITIES

Government programmes for the renewal of the inner cities are carried out by several departments. Since 1988, the work has been conducted under the banner of the 'Action for Cities' initiative. Business has been involved as an essential partner in the process, together with local authorities, the voluntary sector and local people.

Within Whitehall, the DOE has a co-ordinating role and provides the bulk of the financial resources deployed.

The Government works with business primarily through the following programmes:

- A range of training and enterprise programmes (plus schools/industry compacts or agreed programmes of collaboration) delivered by the Training and Enterprise Councils. These include Employment Training, the Youth Training Scheme, the Enterprise Allowance Scheme, and the Small Firms Service (Employment Department)
- A range of employment programmes operated by the Employment Service, including Jobcentres, Jobclubs, and Job interview guarantee schemes (Employment Department)
- Renewal programmes delivered via the Urban Development Corporations (Department of the Environment)
- City Grant, to compensate developers for the extra costs of building in inner cities (Department of the Environment)
- Regional Enterprise Grants, to encourage investment and innovation by small businesses (Department of Trade and Industry)

The Government works with local authorities primarily through the following programmes:

- The Urban Programme, with economic, social, environmental and housing objectives (Department of the Environment)
- Estate Action, with the objective of improving the worst local authority estates (Department of the Environment)
- Housing Investment Programmes, including special allocations to direct additional housing investment towards inner city authorities, plus the special homelessness initiative (Department of the Environment)
- Derelict Land Grant, to restore damaged sites to a usable state (Department of the Environment)
- Transport Supplementary Grant, to aid road building (Department of Transport)
- Section II grants, to tackle ethnic minority needs in education, social services, enterprise support and other areas (Home Office)

The Government works with the voluntary sector and community groups primarily through:

- Its training and employment programmes (nationally a substantial proportion of places on training programmes are now provided by voluntary sector training agents)
- Support for housing associations (given via the Housing Corporation)
- The Urban Programme (a quarter of the total expenditure goes on voluntary projects)

The Government has also set up two key mechanisms to help in focusing its programmes on priority areas:

- City Action Teams
- Task Forces

City Action Teams

Eight City Action Teams have been established to co-ordinate government action at local level. They consist of the senior regional officials of the Departments of Environment, Trade and Industry and Employment, plus officials from other departments as necessary. Their task is to ensure that the individual departmental programmes are working together effectively on the ground. They act as a central contact point with government for business and community organizations. Each CAT has a small special budget for tackling local inner city problems which relate to unemployment, enterprise generation and environmental improvement.

Task Forces

Task Forces are operated by the DTI. They cover smaller areas than the City Action Teams – say the area of a council estate – and are temporary in nature. Although there are 16 Task Forces, since March 1989 six have been closed and six opened in other areas. In addition to their own funds, Task Forces seek to attract contributions from other public and private sources.

8
Department of Transport

The Department of Transport is of major importance to business both directly, as regulator of the many businesses within the sector, as major client of the construction industry through its roadbuilding, and as a provider of many services; and indirectly, since transport of people and goods is a vital input to businesses of all kinds.

With a staff of 16,000 and an annual budget of £5.2 billion, the Department has extensive responsibilities over all modes of transport. It is one of the most 'hands-on' or action-oriented of all Whitehall departments. Fully 90 per cent of its staff work outside London, in regional offices or specialist organizations such as the Driver and Vehicle Licensing Centre in Swansea (4,000 staff), providing services or performing direct executive functions in the areas of safety, security, etc.

Those parts of the Department providing services to the public were therefore prime candidates to become executive agencies, and indeed the Vehicle Inspectorate was the first such agency to be formed, in August 1988, followed by the Driving Standards Agency, the Vehicle Certification Agency, the Driver and Vehicle Licensing Agency and the Transport and Road Research Laboratory. Thus 60 per cent of the Department's staff is now in agencies.

The Department (see Figure 8.1) is organized broadly vertically into the four main transport modes, and its main responsibilities are:

ROAD

- Direct responsibility for constructing and maintaining motorways and trunk roads, and oversight of local authority responsibilities for other

Figure 8.1 Organization of the Department of Transport

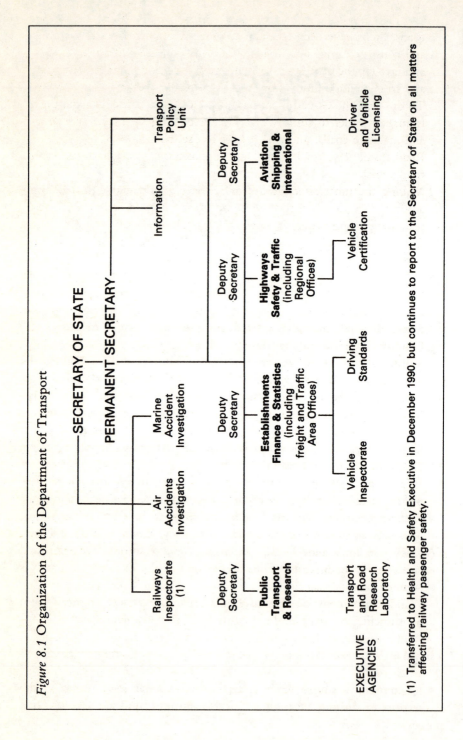

SECRETARY OF STATE

PERMANENT SECRETARY

Railways Inspectorate (1)

Air Accidents Investigation

Marine Accident Investigation

Information

Transport Policy Unit

Deputy Secretary

Deputy Secretary

Deputy Secretary

Deputy Secretary

Public Transport & Research

Establishments Finance & Statistics (including freight and Traffic Area Offices)

Highways Safety & Traffic (including Regional Offices)

Aviation Shipping & International

EXECUTIVE AGENCIES

Transport and Road Research Laboratory

Vehicle Inspectorate

Driving Standards

Vehicle Certification

Driver and Vehicle Licensing

(1) Transferred to Health and Safety Executive in December 1990, but continues to report to the Secretary of State on all matters affecting railway passenger safety.

roads. Steps have been taken to involve private firms in the financing and construction of new roads, as already happens with bridges. The aim is to tap the private sector's entrepreneurial and management skills, and to encourage innovation in a traditionally public sector domain. To this end, the Government has introduced new procedures designed to make it easier to authorize private sector firms to finance, construct and maintain roads, and charge tolls to use them.

- Road traffic law, road safety, and the taxation, safety and testing of road vehicles
- Making the most effective use of roads, e.g., through research into automatic incident detection on motorways and the installation of new technology to improve the capacity of junctions
- The licensing and testing of drivers, the licensing of lorry and bus operators and the registration of bus services

RAIL

- Setting financial and service targets and grant levels for British Rail and London Underground, approving their strategic plans and considering individual major investment proposals
- The regulation of railway safety
- The encouragement of rail use, where this secures environmental benefits by keeping lorries off unsuitable roads, through grants to companies changing from road to rail, or to local authorities promoting light rail systems in their areas
- Oversight of the national interest in the Channel Tunnel project
- British Rail has been asked by the Department to broaden private sector participation in the provision of services to the railway, and the following examples illustrate the possibilities:
  - a joint venture project has been developed for a new Heathrow Express Link and there have been major property developments involving the private sector at stations
  - many ancillary services such as on-train catering, parcels deliveries and management of some car parks are now privately operated
  - following the privatization of British Rail Engineering Ltd (BREL), all rolling stock is now bought from the private sector and privately owned wagons account for 39 per cent of the total wagon fleet.

In addition, of course, the privatization of British Rail is planned, but at the time of writing (March 1992) the form and timing had not been announced.

AIR

The Department is responsible for Government policy with regard to airports, airspace and air traffic control, competition between British airlines, aircraft noise and other environmental matters, investigation of air accidents, the financing of search and rescue services and certain research and development programmes.

Much of the detailed economic and safety regulation of the civil aviation sector is delegated to the Civil Aviation Authority (CAA), an independent statutory body whose board is appointed by the Secretary of State for Transport. The CAA is responsible for ensuring that British airlines provide services to satisfy all main categories of customer at lowest charges consistent with high safety standards. It also provides air traffic control services jointly with the Ministry of Defence. The CAA contains a Safety Regulation Group, concerned with all aspects of aviation safety, including the certification of aircraft and licensing of crews, and an Economic Regulation Group, concerned with route licensing and air fares.

The main functions retained within the Department are:

- *Aviation security*: though security measures are implemented by the airports and airlines, the Department sets standards and conducts inspections to ensure they are followed
- *Airports policy*: especially planning for future capacity needs, and including the control of capital investment at local authority airports. A working group has been commissioned to examine the wider implications of providing the runway capacity in locations which the CAA has advised are feasible in air traffic control terms. It will, in particular, examine the degree to which the regions may be able to relieve the pressure of demand on the South East
- *Airline competition*
- *International air service agreeements*: Department officials negotiate bilateral and multilateral international agreements to provide traffic rights for air services to and from the UK
- *Aircraft noise*: Department officials negotiate with the International Civil Aviation Organization to establish international noise standards for most types of aircraft. In the UK, the Department imposes controls directly at Heathrow, Gatwick and Stansted through, for example, restrictions on night flights

SEA

- International negotiations to remove protectionist restrictions on British shipping
- The privatization of the Trust Ports
- The maintenance of ship safety through international agreements and, domestically, the setting and enforcement of standards for UK-registered ships. The Surveyor General's organization regulates the construction, maintenance and safe operation of ships and their equipment, and sponsors research into ship safety
- Ensuring safety of navigation through traffic separation schemes in UK waters, providing aids to navigation, and administering a consent procedure for the construction of works in tidal waters
- The investigatory and emergency services of:
  - HM Coastguard
  - Marine Accidents Investigation Branch
  - Marine Pollution Control Unit
- Assistance to the shipping industry: the Department administers a number of measures to assist in the recruitment, training and employment of British seafarers. Schemes have been established:
  - to assist with the costs of transporting crews to and from ships operating in distant waters
  - to meet half the costs of training officer cadets
  - to create and maintain a Merchant Navy Reserve designed to provide a pool of experienced ex-seafarers for crewing merchant ships in crisis and war

In September 1990, a report, *British Shipping: Challenges and Opportunities*, was published following a joint government/industry working party. It made several recommendations including rules governing officer nationality and the registration of vessels in the UK, liberalization in Europe, and further incentives to encourage recruitment and training, all of which are being pursued by Government and the industry.

CENTRAL SERVICES AND RESEARCH

Backing up the basically modal organization of the Department are units looking at issues, e.g., the environment, which affect more than one mode, transport in London, and economic and statistical experts. The Transport and Road Research Laboratory at Crowthorne (600 staff) undertakes scientific research which enables the Department to set standards for highway and vehicle design, formulate road safety policies and encourage good traffic engineering practice.

CONTACT POINTS

For most businesspeople with an enquiry on transport matters in England, the DTp's regional offices in the English regions will be the first source of information (details are published in the *Civil Service Year Book*). They have expanded their traditional role of managing road schemes in their areas and now cover all aspects of transport. In addition, they work closely with local authorities and other government departments, especially the Department of the Environment, where the two Departments have joint regional offices and regional directors. There is also increasing regional liaison with the Department of Trade and Industry, especially on inner city regeneration activities.

A list of contact points, including telephone numbers, in the central department and executive agencies, is published in the Department's Annual Report.

9
The Treasury
(including Inland Revenue
and HM Customs and
Excise)

As well as the Treasury, Inland Revenue and Customs, the Chancellor of the Exchequer is responsible for eight other departments, including, for example, the Department for National Savings and the Central Office of Information. Further, within HM Treasury, there is Central Treasury (the policy arm), plus three 'businesses' – the Chessington Computer Centre which is a major provider of payroll and allied services to government departments, the Civil Service Catering Organization, and the Central Computing and Telecommunications Agency (CCTA).

In the description which follows, a selection has been made from amongst all those activities to illuminate the areas of greatest relevance to business.

Central Treasury: Influencing policies for business

Central Treasury is responsible for overall financial and economic policy, the control of public expenditure, and civil service management and pay. Its senior management structure is set out in Figure 9.1. Despite its importance, it is a small department by Whitehall standards – some 1,400 strong. When secretarial and support staff of various kinds are deducted, and those working on civil service pay, etc., there are 68 staff engaged in analysing and forecasting economic developments, and some 395 responsible for planning and controlling £205 bn of public expenditure. It is in

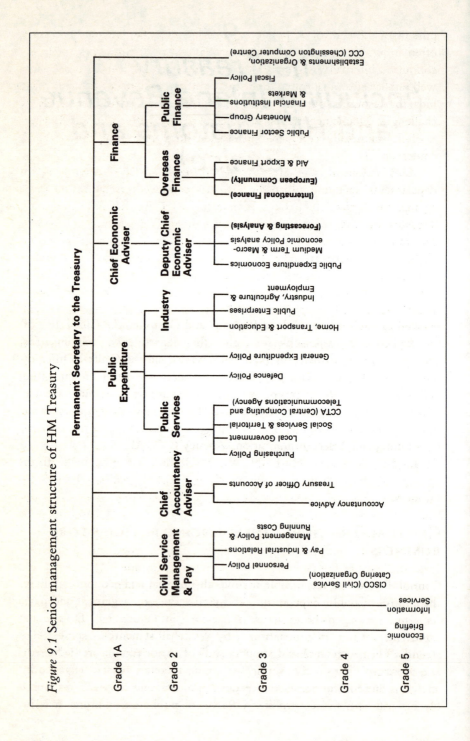

Figure 9.1 Senior management structure of HM Treasury

pursuit of the control of public expenditure that the Treasury will most often impact on policies affecting business, though this work is largely conducted internally within Whitehall. The tip of the iceberg is seen in a well publicized annual round in the early autumn, where departments make bids for resources over the following three years, which the Treasury challenges. Titanic negotiating sessions take place with spending Ministers – often colourfully conducted in seaside hotel bedrooms during Party conference.

Less colourful, and less well-publicized, is the monitoring of departments' spending which the Treasury conducts throughout the year, against the limits which have been established. To do this effectively, Treasury officials must follow closely individual departments' spending programmes; and indeed, they need to be in a position knowledgeably to challenge any departmental policy proposals which may have expenditure implications (as most have). Therefore, within any internal Whitehall inter-departmental machinery, there will almost always be a Treasury representative, whose prime motivation will be to seek economies and challenge new spending proposals.

Thus the various schemes under which the DTI or Department of Employment, etc., convey public funds to business for a whole range of purposes will come under constant scrutiny from the Treasury. Given the enormous imbalance between the number of Treasury officials and the number of those employed in the spending departments, people may ask how the Treasury can carry out an effective scrutiny. Part of the answer was revealed in leaked correspondence between the Treasury and the Department of Employment, in September 1991. The Treasury challenged the expenditure proposals of the Department, the Chief Secretary being quoted as observing that there was no automatic link between higher unemployment and the need for further government provision for training. In other words, the Treasury challenge can, and often does, go back to first principles – to the premise on which policies are based, or to the basic priorities within the Government's overall programme. It does not, and cannot, second guess the dynamics of every scheme within every programme of every department. Out of this process, a sort of rough justice emerges in terms of the aggregate of deals struck between the Treasury and departments. But, of course, the roughness rather than the justice will be seen by business adherents or beneficiaries of a particular scheme which is axed or cut.

It is difficult for businesses to participate in what is, par excellence, a process of the machinery of central government; one, moreover, which is often conducted at great speed and always, leaks notwithstanding, in Whitehall 'family confidence'. Outside of the particularly frenetic atmosphere of the public expenditure round, however, it is possible and desirable to meet and brief Treasury officials on issues of the day that impact on business. It should always be understood, however, that just as with any financial control department, there will be a permanent tension between the Treasury and the department which is closest to the business in policy responsibility. Businesses should try to see the overall political context in which their particular dealings with departments will be seen by the Treasury and be ready to help the former with evidence on cost effectiveness and the other shibboleths normally embraced by finance directors.

BUDGET REPRESENTATIONS – LOBBYING THE REVENUE

The prime impact of government on business is through taxes and duties levied, in the construction of which Treasury Ministers are advised by the Inland Revenue.

Every year, the Budget Statement and ensuing Finance Bill gives government and business alike an opportunity to consider additions, subtractions, or modifications to the fiscal regime surrounding business. Over the years, the Inland Revenue has evolved a procedure which enables business, principally through representative organizations, to make their input to the Budget-making process. The main representative bodies would include the Confederation of British Industry, Institute of Directors, Association of British Chambers of Commerce and trade associations covering particular sectors. In submitting their views to the Chancellor many of the representative bodies distinguish between their main policy representations and their 'technical' suggestions. The former category covers such matters as the appropriate levels of main tax rates and allowances. The technical representations cover a large number and wide range of suggestions. At one extreme they may be concerned with putting right a perceived anomaly affecting only a handful of taxpayers; at the other, with substantial structural changes to the tax system which, though technical in the sense of complex, would also have a significant impact on the yield and distribution of tax. During the autumn the deputy chairmen of the Inland Revenue meet members of some of the main representative bodies and the main accountancy bodies to discuss their technical representations. This enables the Inland Revenue to understand their points more clearly, the extent to which real difficulties are being caused for their members and their order of priorities in seeking changes. In return, the Department explains questions of policy and the technical and operational considerations raised by the proposals and, where points have already been considered by ministers, to give some indication of their views. Similar meetings take place at under secretary and assistant secretary level to examine representations relating to some particular area of taxation rather than the whole field of direct taxes.

These regular discussions have been increasingly supplemented in recent years by formal consultation on particular topics through Green Papers, consultative documents and the publication of draft clauses. In the case of major issues, a select committee may also consider the proposals. These enable Treasury Ministers to obtain the considered views of interested parties in forming their own views and taking decisions on important topic and, in the case of draft clauses, allow extra consideration to be given to detailed drafting of often complex pieces of legislation before the formal legislative process is started. This kind of consultation is inevitably a fairly long drawn out process, particularly where a consultative document discussing the policy issues is followed by the issue of draft clauses embodying Ministers' policy proposals. For this reason it is especially suitable for topics which are of wide general interest but on which legislation is not particularly urgent.

A week or so after publication of the Finance Bill (usually about a month after the Budget) the deputy chairmen of the Inland Revenue hold a Finance Bill 'open day' at which members of some of the main representative bodies ask each of the assistant secretaries in turn factual questions about the meaning and effect of any parts of the Bill they have found unclear.

Within a few weeks of publication another major round of consultation is under way. The pattern is similar to that in the autumn with the deputy chairmen meeting some of the main representative bodies who wish to make more detailed comments across the whole range of the Finance Bill proposals, and other officials generally meeting organizations which are mainly concerned with particular provisions or a more limited range of provisions. Treasury Ministers hold some meetings themselves and officials prepare background briefing and attend to give support if required. At a suitable point a report is made to the Treasury Ministers on all the comments made on a particular provision together with advice on what action, if any, seems appropriate.

There is no 'close season' for considering possible measures for the Finance Bill. Each Finance Bill produces its own unfinished business. As soon as the Bill is passed, therefore, consideration will start to be given to questions raised during the passage of the Bill which may call for legislation the following year. And, by this time, some preliminary thought will already have been given to possible topics for the following year's Budget and Finance Bill. The position has not been altered by the proposals made in March 1992 that, in future, tax and spending proposals should be presented at the same time, in December.

Clearly, then, businesses should take advantage of the procedures which have been set up with CBI, IOD and trade associations to pursue their concerns about taxes. This does not prevent individual companies from making representations, and some of the very big companies, e.g., in the oil industry, regularly do so. But smaller companies, worried perhaps about the particular incidence of a particular tax provision on their business should not feel inhibited about raising the matter. Your accountant, through his professional body, will be able to establish the precise division dealing with the subject.

BUSINESS AND THE TAXMAN

Businesses will have dealings with Inland Revenue local offices in connection with their own tax liability as a business (income tax, Schedule D if the business is unincorporated; corporation tax for incorporated businesses) and in connection with their liability to account for the PAYE deducted from the pay of their employees.

Tax offices are responsible for a particular geographic area, either in part of towns or cities in urban locations, or a part of a county in more rural areas. The tax office dealing with the tax liability of a particular business is generally the one in which the registered office is located (in the case of companies) or in which the main business is conducted (in the case of unincorporated businesses). The tax office dealing with the PAYE responsibilities of a business is the one responsible for the area in which the business's main paying point for employees is situated. Most businesses will have an accountant who will know the appropriate tax office, but in case of doubt, you should look up Inland Revenue in the telephone directory and then contact one of the tax districts listed for the area, who will be pleased to assist.

Inland Revenue tax offices try to provide a good service to taxpayers. If there are problems, the first person to contact is the District Inspector of the office concerned who can sort out most difficulties. If you remain dissatisfied, you should contact the Regional Controller responsible for that tax district.

10
Competition Bodies: Office of Fair Trading; Monopolies and Mergers Commission; and the Utility Regulators

The Secretary of State for Trade and Industry has overall responsibility for UK competition policy. The two main official bodies which deal with competition matters, and complementary consumer protection duties, are the Office of Fair Trading (OFT) and the Monopolies and Mergers Commission (MMC). The Secretary of State appoints the Director-General of the OFT and the chairmen and members of the MMC, but the two organizations are separate, and independent of government. Neither the Director-General of the OFT nor the Chairman or members of the MMC are civil servants, but most of their staff are.

The roles and responsibilities of the Secretary of State, the OFT and the MMC, with regard to various aspects of competition, are laid down in law. The principal acts are the Fair Trading Act 1973, the Restrictive Trade Practices Act 1976, the Resale Prices Act 1976 and the Competition Act 1980. However, subsequent legislation dealing principally with the privatization of public utilities has added new responsibilities to both bodies.

In general terms, the OFT is the mainspring of the system. It monitors the whole scene from a competitive and consumer standpoint, conducts initial enquiries, 'commissions' detailed investigations by the MMC, advises the Secretary of State generally and monitors and polices undertakings given and regulations made. It also maintains the Register of Restrictive Trading Agreements and may refer restrictive agreements to the Restrictive Practices Court. The MMC is primarily an investigatory body, concerned with establishing the facts and determining whether situations it is called upon to investigate are in the public interest. It does not have the executive role of the OFT.

OFFICE OF FAIR TRADING

The overall objective of the OFT is to advance and protect the economic interests of consumers. It ensures there is effective competition in the marketplace, promotes consumer education and enforces regulations designed to counter specific unfair practices. In addition to the duties laid down for the OFT in legislation, Ministers may and do ask the OFT to investigate particular issues, e.g., estate agents or timeshare companies; and the OFT itself can decide to study a particular sector of trading practice and propose action. One of the best-known functions of the OFT is to advise the Secretary of State on whether to refer apparent monopoly situations, whether or not arising from a proposed merger, to the MMC for investigation. The MMC itself has no powers to initiate such investigations (see below). Finally, the OFT is the 'competent authority' (with the DTI) for assisting the European Commission in applying the EC's competition rules in the UK.

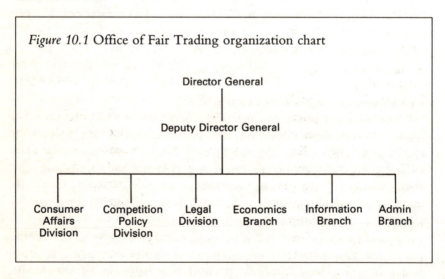

Figure 10.1 Office of Fair Trading organization chart

Director General

Deputy Director General

| Consumer Affairs Division | Competition Policy Division | Legal Division | Economics Branch | Information Branch | Admin Branch |

The two main operating arms of the OFT are Consumer Affairs Division and Competition Policy Division. The following examples of their work illustrate the extremely wide canvas of the department.

Consumer affairs

This Division is responsible for reviewing and reporting on trade practices, publishing information for consumers, encouraging codes of practice, and acting against traders who persistently break the law. It also issues licenses for consumer credit agencies and polices regulations governing estate agents.

For example, the Division monitors the working of codes of practice such as those of the National Association of Funeral Directors. It then makes recommendations to improve the treatment the public receives from these industries, e.g., information on prices.

In the field of consumer education, a wide range of practical leaflets is published, e.g., on buying used cars or obtaining copies of entries in credit reference agency files. Material is also generated for use in schools.

The Division makes extensive use of surveys and consultative documents and is the recipient of many complaints about trading practices (2,000 letters on time-share alone). Much of its work is conducted in conjunction with trade associations and local authority trading standards officers.

Traders who persistently break the law to the detriment of consumers, e.g., by making false statements, can be asked to give assurances to the Director-General of the OFT on their future good conduct. If these assurances are broken, the Director-General can bring proceedings to obtain a court order, breach of which can be held to be contempt of court.

Competition policy

This Division has a high profile role, dealing with monopolies, mergers, restrictive trade practices and anti-competition practices generally. It has special responsibilities under the Financial Services Act 1986, and is the contact point for the European Commission on competition matters. The OFT continually monitors the whole of industry and commerce with special attention being paid to large companies. Allegations of monopoly abuse – or other anti-competitive practices – are investigated. In the case of mergers, although companies are not obliged to inform the Office of their plans, many do so. There is an informal confidential guidance procedure, where companies contemplating a merger or takeover can be given guidance on whether a reference to the MMC is likely. In 1989 there were

32 applications for confidential guidance. Of these, 18 received favourable and four unfavourable guidance. Guidance was withheld in the remaining 10 cases. In addition, the Companies Act 1989 introduced a formal procedure for companies to pre-notify a merger to the Office, which can lead to rapid clearance.

The procedures for investigating monopolies and mergers are very similar. The OFT may itself refer a monopoly situation to the MMC for investigation; in the case of mergers, the procedure is to advise the Secretary of State (of the DTI) to refer. In either case, the MMC conducts a detailed examination and submits a report to the Secretary of State, who will take a decision on the matter with the advice of the OFT. Similarly, it will be for the OFT to follow-up if necessary, to obtain undertakings from the parties concerned and ensure they are honoured. A well-publicized example of this process was the MMC investigation into the supply of beer, which reported in 1989 and recommended structural changes in the industry. In summary, the major brewers were eventually compelled to divest themselves of many of their tied pubs and to allow their tied tenants freedom to buy some beers from other suppliers. It is the OFT which is charged with ensuring compliance with these orders and reporting on how effective they are in increasing competition.

Companies colluding to make restrictive agreements, e.g., on pricing or market share, are obliged to register such agreements with the OFT, and it is the duty of the OFT, on investigation, normally to refer these to the Restrictive Practices Court which will strike down any restriction found to be against the public interest. The Director-General has the discretion to advise that insignificant restrictions need not be referred to the Court.

There are all sorts of particular activities by individual companies which may be anti-competitive but do not merit the detailed and time consuming process of an MMC investigation. This might include, for example, predatory pricing on a bus route or the refusal of a manufacturer to supply certain retailers, or the imposition of conditions that retailers should not do business with competitors of the manufacturer. The Competition Act 1980 gave the OFT powers to conduct investigations into such practices. Most investigations arise from complaints received in the Office from those affected. If, on enquiry, the complaints appear to have substance, a small team is appointed to handle the case, the investigation having been announced publicly to all those who might have an interest. The OFT can require anyone to provide documents or information, but there are restrictions on what might subsequently be published.

The Office then produces a report stating whether an anti-competitive practice has been identified. If so, it may be referred to the MMC or the OFT may deal with it. Again, the process of obtaining and policing undertakings on future conduct comes into play.

The Financial Services Act 1976 and the Companies Act 1989 created a new regulatory regime for the financial services industry. Under the former act, the Director-General of Fair Trading examines the rules of the financial self-regulatory bodies from a competition standpoint and monitors their operation.

Relations with the European Commission

The EC rules on competition are directly applicable in the UK and the European Commission is directly responsible for ensuring their application. However, the OFT, as a 'competent authority', is deeply involved in any such casework. For example, a member of OFT staff would always accompany Commission inspectors making visits to UK companies during their investigations. Similarly, OFT staff attend hearings in Brussels when British companies accused of infringing EC competition rules defend themselves. There is a wide range of formal and informal contacts between the OFT and the Commission, especially the Directorate-General for Competition (DG IV). The OFT can advise companies on correct procedures to follow when approaching the Commission on competition matters.

Getting in touch

The OFT is interested in getting the facts right and arriving at a correct understanding of the business sector it monitors. It obviously would wish to be informed of anti-competitive behaviour, wherever it occurs; but equally is willing to give informal and confidential advice to companies contemplating mergers or takeovers.

Monopolies and Mergers Commission

The MMC was established in 1948, but its modern role was expanded and re-defined in the 1973 and 1980 Acts referred to previously, and in the various pieces of legislation in the 1980s privatizing several utilities, such as telecommunications, gas etc. Its findings can have a considerable impact on business, and its activities – especially with regard to proposed mergers – can have a high profile. Though linked to, it is not part of, government. It cannot operate on its own initiative, but only when invited to do so by the Secretary of State (DTI) or, more commonly, the Director-General of the OFT. Its basic function is investigative – to establish the facts of a referred situation and come to a judgment as to whether the situation operates in the public interest or not. This entails a detailed, and often time-consuming process; but its reports, which are always published are authoritative, and its public interest judgments, on the occasions when they have been made subject to judicial review, have never been overturned.

The 35 members of the Commission are appointed for a renewable three-year term by the Secretary of State for the DTI, which finances the Commission. Only the chairman is full-time, but all are paid. (See Annexe at the end of this chapter for the names and backgrounds of the Commission in 1991.) They are senior and experienced figures drawn from business, academic and similar backgrounds, often with legal and financial expertise. When a reference is made to the MMC, the chairman chooses a group of four to six members, chaired usually by himself or one of his two deputies, to conduct the enquiry. The deputy chairmen work two and a half days per week and members one and a half days per week, enabling them to participate in two concurrent references.

The Commission is supported by some 110 staff, who are organized into groups of teams conducting enquiries and advisory divisions structured on a professional functional basis (see Figure 10.2). When the chairman chooses his group of members to conduct an enquiry, the secretary appoints a team manager reporting to the chairman of the group and leading a team with the appropriate balance of economic and accountancy skills, drawing on other specialist advice within the Commission and occasionally from outside advisers. The Reference Secretary is the focal point of contact within the Commission and with outside parties.

The main types of references to the MMC have been and still are:

- Mergers
- Monopolies
- Competition
- Public sector

but, in recent years, a new category has been added:

- Privatization, i.e., provisions for references to be made in the privatized areas of telecommunications, gas, airports, water and electricity, to establish whether those new private organizations licensed to provide a monopolistic service are operating in the public interest

- Plus, most recently, a role under the Broadcasting Act 1990 to investigate the competitive aspects of networking agreements between holders of new commercial television (Channel 3) franchises.

In 1990, the 35 references completed by the MMC fell into the following pattern:

Mergers	27
Monopolies	5
Competition	1
Public sector	2

The work of the MMC reflects trends outside its control, e.g., privatizations, the desire of companies to expand by organic growth rather than acquisition etc. However, in most recent years, mergers have been the main type of reference. Many businesses will find themselves, or their competitors or suppliers on one or the other side of a bid, leading to a proposed merger. There is therefore much interest, and a good deal of ill-informed speculation about what sort of 'lobbying' is appropriate or possible, particularly during a contested bid.

All the publicity and special pleading should not be allowed to obscure two fundamental facts. First, most proposed mergers do in fact go through (about three-quarters of the mergers considered by the OFT in any year are held not to raise significant public interest issues). Second, those which are referred are, in the great majority of cases, referred because they appear to be restricting competition and for no other reason.

In a non-contested bid, the interest of the parties involved in the merger is to present their case in such a way that the Director-General of Fair Trading does not refer it to the MMC. By contrast, in a contested bid, the objective of the target company is to secure a referral, since under the City code this means the predator's bid must lapse, thus enabling the target time to build up his defence.

In either case, as mentioned previously, it is open for any of the parties involved, prior to their intentions being made public, to seek informal and confidential guidance from the OFT as to whether the merger is likely to be referred. Strictly, the guidance is from the Secretary of State, on the advice of the OFT. This confidential guidance is available on the basis that it remains confidential, i.e., unrevealed by the parties concerned, when the bid is made public. It should be noted that when the OFT withholds guidance, as distinct from giving favourable or unfavourable guidance, it

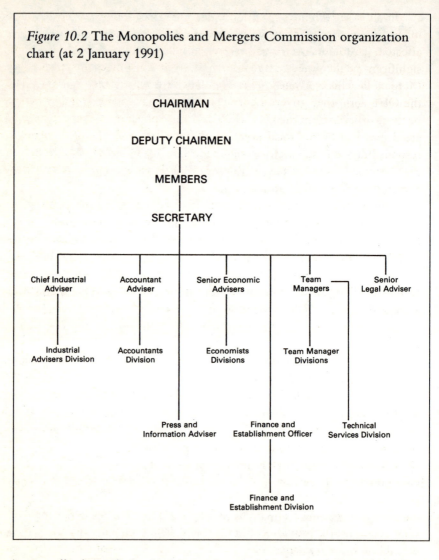

Figure 10.2 The Monopolies and Mergers Commission organization chart (at 2 January 1991)

is normally due to lack of information on which to base a judgment, rather than necessarily a view that the judgment will be finely balanced.

The Companies Act 1989 introduced a new procedure for voluntarily pre-notifying publicly-announced mergers to the OFT (there is no legal obligation to do so other than for newspapers). Upon supplying relevant information, and subject to certain exceptions, such mergers are automatically cleared at the end of a certain period if the OFT has not made a reference to the MMC.

In all cases, whether pre-notified or not, once the merger proposal is made public the OFT will seek comments from those who would be affected (customers, competitors etc.). When there appears to be some significant public interest issue involved, a Whitehall mechanism called the Mergers Panel is convened. This consists of a group of civil servants from the OFT and other government departments. The main attendees would be those officials from the DTI, DTp or other 'sponsoring' department who are deemed to be the focal point of Whitehall knowledge of, and policy responsibility for, the sector concerned. The job of the Panel is to advise the Director-General of the OFT prior to his decision on how to advise the Secretary of State on referral.

This is the focal point which should not be missed by those businesses affected by the proposed merger, in whatever capacity, who wish to make their views known. Even if the OFT has been in touch directly, if a company feels strongly that issues of importance to their area of industry are raised by the proposed merger, it should ensure that the appropriate sector of DTI or other 'sponsoring' ministry is briefed, since this will ensure a separate input into the Mergers Panel.

Lobbying on bids

Some target companies of hostile bids decide, or are badly advised, to conduct a political lobbying campaign at this stage against the bid, in the hope of achieving referral. MPs are circulated with defence documents, meetings are arranged, perhaps questions or motions are contrived. None of this has any effect on the decision-making process within the OFT, though it may bolster the morale of the target company – at a cost. The OFT proceeds through rational evaluation of individual cases, with the effect on competition the primary consideration, on the basis of evidence put to it or unearthed by it.

Target companies would therefore be better advised to concentrate their resources on providing the OFT and their sponsor department with detailed factual guidance on the likely diminution of competition in particular product and market segments. On the other hand, acquiring companies are entitled to put such arguments into perspective; competition in markets is seldom just an arithmetical matter of market share, but this is the sort of argument which in practice is more likely to be addressed by the MMC. If there is a *prima facie* case of competition being restricted, the presumption must be that the OFT will refer the case to the Commission. The point is that this will occur as a result of analysis, not of political lobbying.

ANNEXE

Monopolies and Mergers Commission

Sir Sydney Lipman, *Chairman*. Formerly Deputy Chairman of Allied Dunbar Assurance plc.

Peter Dean, *Deputy Chairman*. Formerly executive Director of the RTZ Corporation plc from 1974 to 1985. He is a solicitor and a non-executive director of Associated British Ports Holdings plc and Liberty Life Assurance Company Ltd.

Holman Hunt CBE, *Deputy Chairman*. Formerly Managing Director of PA Computers and Telecommunications Ltd, a past President of the Institute of Management Consultants. He is also a Fellow of the Institute of Cost and Management Accountants, of the Institute of Administrative Management and of the British Computer Society.

Hans Liesner CB, *Deputy Chairman*. Former civil servant (Deputy Secretary, DTI, responsible for competition matters).

Colin Baillieu. Formerly Chairman and Managing Director of Ultrasonic Machines. Chairman of Gresham Underwriting Agencies Ltd.

Ian Barter. Fellow of King's College, Cambridge. Former Director of Unigate plc. Barrister.

Professor Michael Beesley, CBE. Professor of Economics at London Business School and economic adviser to Government in various capacities, including privatization.

Catherine M. Blight. A solicitor and economist and part-time lecturer at the University of Edinburgh.

Frederick Bonner CBE. Formerly Deputy Chairman of the Central Electricity Generating Board. Non-executive Director of Nuclear Electric plc. Chartered Accountant.

Patrick Brenan. An accountant and financial consultant. Chairman of the London Italian Bank.

John S. Bridgeman. Managing Director of the Enterprises Division of British Alcan Aluminium plc.

Lewis Britz. Executive Councillor of the Electrical, Electronic, Communications and Plumbing Union, for dealing with Ford Motor Company and British Airways. Director of British International Helicopters.

Keith Carmichael CBE. Formerly managing partner of Longcrofts, Chartered Accountants.

Roger Davies. Formerly Chairman of the Thomson Travel Group.

Professor Sam Eilon. A management consultant and Senior Research Fellow at Imperial College.

James Evans. A Director of Reuters and of Thomson Regional Newspapers. A lawyer. He was a member of the Franks Committee on the Official Secrets Act.

Alexander Ferry MBE. General Secretary of the Confederation of Shipbuilding and Engineering Unions. Non-Executive Director of Harland and Wolff Shipbuilders.

Dan Goyder. A solicitor specializing in competition law.

Michael Hoffman. Group Chief Executive of Thames Water plc. He served on the Department of Trade and Industry Technical Requirements Board and the British Overseas Trade Board.

James Keir QC. Formerly Joint Secretary of Unilever and head of the company's legal service. He is Chairman of the Pharmacists' Review Panel.

Leonard Kingshott. A Director of the Crown Agents. Formerly Director of International Banking at Lloyds Bank and has also been with Ford, British Steel and Whitbread.

Patricia Mann. Vice-President International of J. Walter Thompson. A Director of the Woolwich Building Society, Yale and Valor plc. Editor of *Consumer Affairs*.

Graham Mather. Director General of the Institute of Economic Affairs. Previously Head of the Institute of Directors Policy Unit. He is a solicitor.

Leif Mills. General Secretary of the Banking Insurance and Finance Union. Previously a member of the Armed Forces Pay Review body. A Governor of the London Business School and a member of the Financial Reporting Council.

Professor Patrick Minford. Professor of Applied Economics at Liverpool University. An economic adviser to a number of government departments and to Courtaulds Ltd.

John Montgomery. A solicitor and formerly Head of Legal Division and Company Secretary of Shell UK Ltd.

Bernard Owens. A Director of Welsh Water's Land and Leisure Subsidiary and of the Cornish Brewery Company Limited.

Professor John Pickering. Vice-President (Business and Finance) of Portsmouth Polytechnic.

Leslie Priestley. A Board Member of the Civil Aviation Authority and a Director of Pearce Group Holdings plc and London Electricity plc. Formerly Chairman and Chief Executive of TSB England and Wales plc.

David Thomson. Formerly Director-General of the British Invisible Exports Council and a Director of Lazards.

Cyril A. Unwin MBE. Formerly a full-time official of the General and Municipal Workers Union.

Sam Wainwright CBE. Formerly Managing Director of National Girobank plc and a member of the Board of the Post Office.
Professor Geoffrey Whittington. Professor of Financial Accounting at the University of Cambridge. Academic Adviser to the Accounting Standards Board.
Robert Young. Director of Beauford plc, formerly with Vickers and has served in the No 10. Policy Unit and the Central Policy Review Staff.

THE UTILITY REGULATORS

The programme of the Thatcher Administration from 1979 embraced the privatization of various public sector organizations, engaged in the production and sale of goods or services which were felt to be better situated in the private sector. However, some of these, in particular British Telecom, British Gas, the (non-nuclear) electricity generation and supply companies and the water and sewerage undertakings, were monopolies, either nationally or in their regions. Moreover, they were 'natural' monopolies, in the sense that it would have been plainly inefficient to multiply the resources required, say, to supply water on a competitive basis within the Thames area. In general, the pipelines, power lines, etc., of the previous monopoly utilities were a powerful deterrent to the normal entry of competitive suppliers to any market.

It was therefore considered essential to introduce, alongside each privatization, a regulatory regime and authority which would protect consumers against monopolistic exploitation, particularly on pricing, and generally to mimic real life competition.

Thus, there were created, in succession:

1984   Office of Telecommunications (OFTEL)
1986   Office of Gas Supply (OFGAS)
1989   Office of Water Services (OFWAT)
1989   Office of Electricity Regulation (OFFER)

The directors-general appointed came, in two cases, from an academic background; one was a Treasury official and one an accountant. Their staff were drawn from the civil service departments most involved. The precise powers of the respective directors-general of these offices is laid down in the Acts which simultaneously privatized the industries and established the regulatory bodies. The crucial power is over prices charged by the privatized monopolies, but there are added important additional responsibilities, e.g., over energy efficiency and water quality. Other than the privatized public businesses themselves, the interest of businesses generally in these regimes is that of a consumer.

Because it is fundamental to the role of the regulatory bodies to protect the interests of the consumer, it is up to business consumers to contact the regulators if they have unresolved problems with the utilities concerned. Since their respective appointments, the directors-general have demonstrated their total independence from the industries they regulate. A business consumer with an unresolved problem would be well advised to have a discussion with the regulator, although it is obvious that the plight of individual citizens will always be given a powerful emphasis by such agencies, especially in the comparatively early years of their establishment.

11
Ministry of Defence, Procurement Executive

The Procurement Executive (PE) of the MoD is British industry's biggest customer, spending around £8 billion a year on equipment for the armed services, ranging from sophisticated weapons systems to batteries. There are therefore sales opportunities for businesses in all sectors, and of all sizes. The Ministry is keen to expand its list of suppliers and to provide opportunities for small firms as well as the large defence contractors like British Aerospace and GEC. In addition, the Defence Export Services Organization helps UK companies sell their defence products and services overseas.

The thrust of the MoD's procurement policy in recent years has been to obtain better value for money in its purchases by tightening up the terms and conditions under which it does business with its suppliers and by increasing the degree of competition, national and international, for its business.

The results of this policy can be illustrated by the following statistics: over the past eight years the number of contracts placed as a result of competition or by reference to market forces has increased from 38 per cent (by value) to 67 per cent.

The top level organization of the Procurement Executive is shown in Figure 11.1. The PE is headed by the Chief of Defence Procurement (CDP), who chairs the monthly meetings of the Procurement Executive Management Board (PEMB). This is the PE's top level decision-making body responsible for deciding policy and the future direction and strategy of the equipment programme. Down the line, the actual purchasing activities of the MoD are carried out by MoD contracts branches located mainly in London, Bath, Glasgow, Liverpool, Portsmouth and Weymouth;

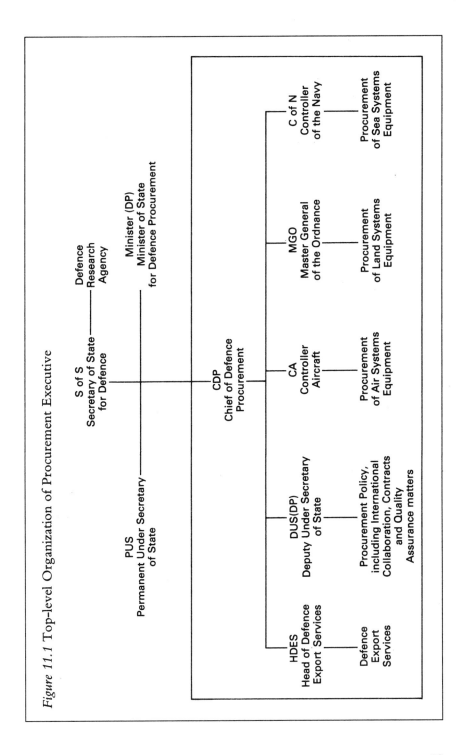

Figure 11.1 Top-level Organization of Procurement Executive

by designated local purchase offices at service units; and of course indirectly via the sub-contracts placed by MoD prime contractors.

In broad outline, the procurement process is triggered off in the following way. The overall shape and size and affordability of the weapons requirement is determined in the department's Office of Management and Budget, based on operational requirements emanating from the armed services. The PE has a stake in decision making, especially on technical requirements, and assesses the feasibility of what the services would like to see. The Ministry's own Defence Research Agency (an executive agency established in April 1991, comprising the Ministry's non-nuclear research establishments) is used to do preparatory research and to assess development work on weapons and defence systems.

Once an equipment requirement has been defined, major projects are subjected to detailed scrutiny by the Equipment Policy Committee, which is chaired by the MoD's Chief Scientific Advisor. The EPC looks at the largest projects (development and production costs in excess of £50 million and £100 million respectively) and makes recommendations to Ministers, with whom the final decisions rest. A project manager will normally be appointed at an early stage in the process and once the project is under way he will be supported by a project team consisting of finance, contracts, technical and quality assurance staff, and others as necessary. Working to the appropriate systems controller, the project manager has overall responsibility for the management of all aspects of the procurement of an equipment item within authorized programme and budget constraints.

Increasing emphasis is given to providing project managers, and their teams, with appropriate training in order for them to operate effectively. Part of this training involves giving managers exposure to a commercial environment and to this end the MoD runs a programme of industrial secondments both inward and outward. In 1990 there were 88 secondments to industry, of which 80 were from the PE. In the opposite direction, merchant bankers have been appointed as advisers on defence exports; also contacts have been established with City analysts.

Consultative machinery has been set up to discuss broad policy issues with the defence supply industry. At top level is the Defence Industries Council consisting of senior representatives from industry, which meets with the Secretary of State twice yearly. The Chief of Defence Procurement also meets twice yearly with the main trade associations in the industry and the CBI.

The European dimension of the MoD is different from other departments, since Article 223 of the Treaty of Rome provides the basis for excluding defence procurement from the ambit of the EC. However, it has come to be accepted by European governments that closer co-operation is desirable on industrial aspects of defence, without encroaching on defence policy questions. The main European forum for the discussion of defence procurement and equipment co-operation is the Independent European Programme Group (IEPG) which comprises the European members of the North Atlantic Alliance. The aim of the group is to promote European collaboration in defence equipment matters in order to permit more effective use of funds for research and development, to increase standardization and interoperability of equipment, to maintain a healthy industrial base in Europe; and to facilitate a realistic 'two-way street' between Europe and North America.

The IEPG functions through three panels, respectively dealing with the areas of operational requirements and equipment programmes; research and technology; and economic matters and policy. A small permanent secretariat, based in Lisbon, provides administrative co-ordination.

The most important element of the IEPG programme is the opening up of the European defence equipment market to contractors from all IEPG nations. All IEPG members now have a functioning focal point within their MoD to provide information and to enable companies to register their interests in becoming suppliers. The UK focal point is the New Suppliers Service. IEPG nations also regularly publish defence contracts bulletins.

Making contact

Details of major MoD contracts are published fortnightly on the MoD's *Contracts Bulletin*. In addition, the MoD publishes a wide range of booklets and guidance notes on various detailed aspects of the procurement process, e.g., quality assurance, tendering procedures, etc. A guide to the process as a whole, with details of other publications, contact names, etc., is *Selling to the Ministry of Defence*, available from:

Ministry of Defence, CS (PS)3, Building 25A, Royal Arsenal West, LONDON SE18 6TJ

The main contact point for firms wishing general advice and guidance on selling to the MoD is:

Ministry of Defence, New Suppliers Service, Lacon House, Theobalds Road, LONDON WC1X 8RY

12
Ministry of Agriculture, Fisheries and Food

MAFF is responsible for agriculture, horticulture and fisheries policies in England and for policies on food safety and quality in the UK, including composition, labelling additives, contaminants and new production processes. It negotiates in the EC on the Common Agricultural and Fisheries Policies and in Single Market matters relating to agriculture, fisheries and food; and is responsible for wider international agricultural and food trade policies.

It is responsible for the protection and enhancement of the countryside and marine environment, for flood defence and other rural issues. It is the licensing authority for veterinary medicines and the registration authority for pesticides. It works to prevent and control animal, plant and fish diseases and provides a wide range of advice and services to farmers and others involved in the food chain.

It is organized (see Figure 12.1) into three main policy directorates:

- Agricultural Commodities, Trade and Food Production
- Food Safety
- Countryside, Marine Environment and Fisheries

plus the Chief Scientific Adviser and Chief Scientists' departments and other central and support services.

There are four Executive Agencies, notably the Agricultural Development and Advisory Service (ADAS), which is the main link between the Ministry and the farmer.

MAFF has 10,000 staff, some 40 per cent of whom are in the professional, technical and scientific grades. About 70 per cent of MAFF's staff work outside London.

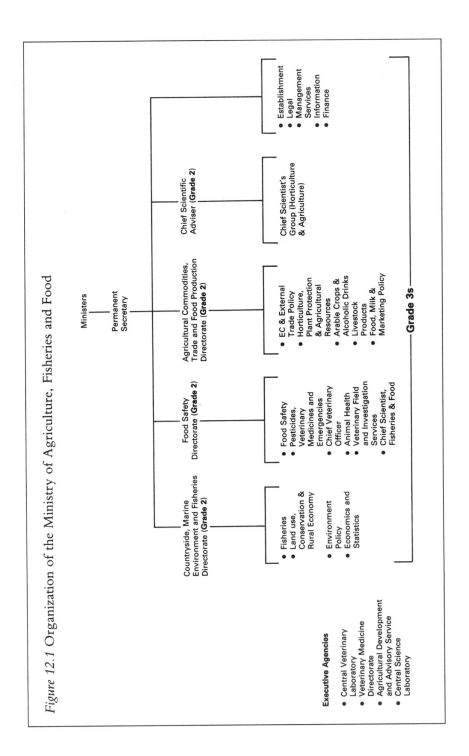

Figure 12.1 Organization of the Ministry of Agriculture, Fisheries and Food

MAFF policies and activities therefore affect a very wide range of businesses in or associated with agriculture, horticulture, fisheries, food and the rural and marine environment. However, its public projection has never done justice to its range of responsibilities, nor, especially in recent years, the balance within those responsibilities. The superficial press and – in some quarters – political jibe that the Department's purpose is to service the farmers' interest is belied by the increasing attention paid to the interests of the consumer and to environmental protection.

With regard to the consumer, the landmark was the Food Safety Act 1990, the first major overhaul of food safety legislation for 35 years. This tightened controls all round, from the registration and licensing of commercial food premises, through contaminants and residues in food, enforcement powers of local authorities, to powers to adapt the law to new technological developments such as cook-chill and irradiation. It made it easier to adapt to the extensive body of food legislation emerging from the EC. Although enforcement of the law is at local level, MAFF's Food Safety Directorate (some 700 strong) provides policy leadership and scientific back-up. Further to strengthen the consumer (as distinct from producer) orientation was the establishment of a consumer panel with representatives from the main consumer organizations, to comment directly to the Food Minister on food safety and consumer protection issues.

Though MAFF has evidently, like every other ministry, responded to increased public awareness of and concern about food safety and the environment, one of its departmental aims remains 'to promote a fair and competitive economy by creating the conditions in which efficient agriculture, fisheries and food industries can flourish'.

This aim is discharged through 15 separate programmes of work documented in the Department's management information system MINIM (Ministerial Information in MAFF) and published by the Department each year as, e.g., MINIM 1990. The 15 programmes concerning the agriculture, fisheries and food industries range from highly specific activities concerning, for example, seed certification or horticultural quality standards inspections to more broadly based promotional activities such as support for Food from Britain. This is a marketing organization founded by both Government and industry which promotes advice and services to help British companies in the food and drink sector to export. In between these two extremes, there are programmes embracing entire food industry sectors, e.g., the operation of the EC fish marketing or wine and spirits regimes.

In general, the department acts as the focus for ensuring that the interests of food and drink manufacturing and distributive industries are taken into account in policy making in Whitehall and Brussels. MAFF will therefore provide representatives to food and drink sector groups in NEDO, will liaise with the trade associations of the sector and will monitor the evolution of competition policy as it affects the sector. It supports the industry in obtaining access to DTI funded aid schemes to encourage firms and research bodies to undertake pre-competitive research on new products and processes, and to selective financial assistance schemes in Assisted Areas.

13
Department
of Energy

The DEn is responsible for national energy policy, including security of supply, energy efficiency, novel forms of energy and international aspects of energy policy. It licenses and regulates the energy industries, especially the offshore oil and gas industry, since the electricity supply industry and British Gas plc are subject to regulation by the Office of Electricity Regulation (OFFER) and the Office of Gas Supply (OFGAS) – see Chapter 10. It funds research and development programmes into various aspects of energy, the bulk of which (around two-thirds) relates to nuclear energy.

It is the sponsoring department for the (private) oil and gas, electricity supply and nuclear power construction industries. Through the Offshore Supplies Office (OSO), it develops the ability of UK suppliers to win business from offshore operators both in the UK and worldwide. It is also responsible for the government relationship with the (public) Nuclear Electric plc, the UK Atomic Energy Authority and British Coal. The organization of the Department – see Figure 13.1 – broadly follows the division of the fuels, plus energy efficiency.

Businesses will therefore be affected by the DEn in three ways:

- As energy consumers
- As energy producers
- As suppliers to the energy industries

ENERGY EFFICIENCY

The prices of oil products are a private sector market matter; those of electricity and gas are regulated by OFFER and OFGAS. The use of energy

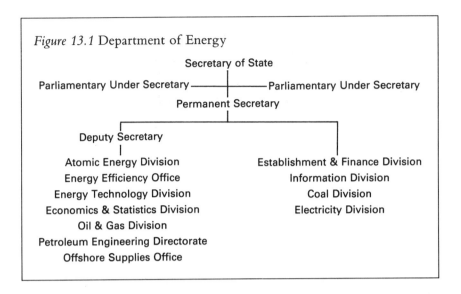

Figure 13.1 Department of Energy

Secretary of State

Parliamentary Under Secretary ————┼———— Parliamentary Under Secretary

Permanent Secretary

Deputy Secretary

Atomic Energy Division
Energy Efficiency Office
Energy Technology Division
Economics & Statistics Division
Oil & Gas Division
Petroleum Engineering Directorate
Offshore Supplies Office

Establishment & Finance Division
Information Division
Coal Division
Electricity Division

is the concern of the Energy Efficiency Office (EEO) within the DEn. The EEO has a budget of around £26 million and offers advice on energy use, backed by technical support. Since its establishment in 1983, the EEO has offered programmes which are claimed to have led to recurrent annual savings of over £500 million a year. Apart from encouraging private households to save energy, the EEO's network of regional energy efficiency officers visit main energy users and assist them in developing energy management programmes.

POLICY TOWARDS INDIVIDUAL FUELS

In broadest terms, the DEn is, at the time of writing (March 1992) preparing the coal industry for privatization; continuing to encourage the exploitation of the oil and gas deposits of the UK Continental Shelf; preparing to review the nuclear reactor building programme in 1994; and researching the technology and clarifying the economics of renewable sources of energy.

Within those generalizations, there are numerous research and development programmes addressing aspects of the various fuels. For example, improving the environmental acceptability of coal utilization; helping to create an advanced UK offshore technological capability; improving oil field safety; maintaining a position in fast reactor technology; improving nuclear safety and radioactive waste management; and detailed investigations into technologies in the fields of solar, wind, tidal and geothermal power.

The Department has, since the mid-1970s, created and managed a regulatory regime for the offshore oil industry. Licences are granted for exploration and production. The development programmes of the oil companies operating offshore will be considered and approved by the Department in some detail and, for example, consents must be obtained for the flaring of associated gas from oil-producing platforms.

OFFSHORE SUPPLIES OFFICE

Although the Department has an interest in all industries supplying the energy sector, it has for many years maintained a special interest in encouraging UK suppliers to have the opportunity to participate in the UK offshore oil industry. This initiative was largely sparked off by the disposition of US oil companies, in the early days of North Sea development, to order all manner of supplies, including nuts and bolts, from their traditional suppliers in the USA.

The Offshore Supplies Office identifies areas of market opportunity for UK suppliers in the UK and overseas and promotes their capability; gives some financial support itself and advises on EC support schemes for the offshore supplies industry; and generally monitors and advises on industrial, technical and financial matters associated with the industry.

14
Department
of Health

The Department of Health impacts upon business directly in three ways:

- The efficiency, quality and safety of the products of the pharmaceutical industry are controlled by the Medicines Control Agency, an executive agency of DH
- The control of the drugs bill to the NHS, and the Government's industrial policy to the pharmaceuticals industry, are the responsibility of the Pharmaceuticals Industry Branch of DH
- The 'supplies' or procurement function of the National Health Service has been centralized in the NHS Supplies Authority, involving the purchase and management of goods and equipment worth over £4 billion

In addition, indirectly, business is affected by the work of the Health Aspects of the Environment and Food Divisions (HEF) of the DH. In policy terms, these cover issues such as irradiation, the microbiological safety of food, imported food regulations, food additives and contaminants, etc.

MEDICINES CONTROL AGENCY (MCA)

The MCA, established in April 1989, protects public health through the regulation and control of medicines, through a system of licensing, classification, monitoring and enforcement under the Medicine Act 1968 and various EC directives. The Agency's 300 plus staff are organized into multi-disciplinary teams in six functional business areas.

The core businesses are concerned with the licensing of medicines containing new chemical entities, involving clinical trials, or 'abridged' licensing of medicines not containing new chemical entities. Other business areas include, for example, the inspection and enforcement business embracing the licensing and inspection of manufacturers and wholesale dealers; defective medicines; and export certificates.

PRICE REGULATION OF THE PHARMACEUTICAL INDUSTRY

The NHS purchases £2 billion worth of branded pharmaceutical products each year. Since 1957 a scheme has been in operation which seeks to ensure that these purchases are made at an acceptable cost to the taxpayer, while observing efficient commercial practices and recognizing the need for continuing research in the pharmaceutical industry.

The Pharmaceutical Price Regulation Scheme (PPRS) controls the price to the NHS of branded products indirectly, through regulating the overall profitability of those supplier companies with sales to the NHS of £500,000 and above. Individual prices are not subject to control. The Scheme is the outcome of negotiations between the DH and the industry; it is not governed by law. Supplier companies are given individual profit targets, based on return on capital or sales, with allowances for research costs specifically provided for. On the other hand, limits are put on the amounts allowable in respect of promotional activities.

The Scheme operates on the basis of an annual cycle of financial information supplied by the companies. Actual profits are compared with the targets and the outcome negotiated. A company may make a case for retaining above-target profits, for example, to fund a new product launch or by demonstrating increased efficiency. This may be accepted, or alternatively the company may have to agree to reduce its prices or make a refund to bring its profits back into line with the target figures.

THE NATIONAL HEALTH SERVICE SUPPLIES AUTHORITY (NHSSA)

The most widespread impact on business by the DH is likely to be made by the new NHS purchasing structure launched in October 1991. Replacing the fragmented system of purchasing by the supplies departments of regional and district health authorities in England, the NHSSA brings the procurement function together in one organization reporting to the NHS management executive.

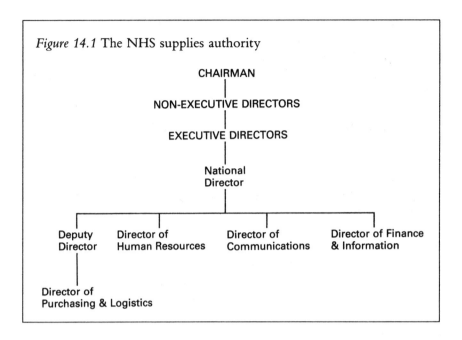

Figure 14.1 The NHS supplies authority

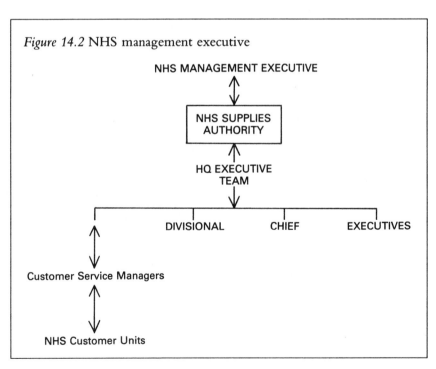

Figure 14.2 NHS management executive

In addition to the increased financial muscle which such an integrated activity can bring to bear in negotiations with suppliers, significant improvements will be sought in information systems, warehousing and distribution.

The NHSSA will be second only to the MoD Procurement Executive in public sector purchasing, with a spend of £4 billion, and a staff of 5,000 controlling purchases from 20,000 suppliers. The Authority will contract with NHS customers – hospitals, community services and health authorities – for the provision of a complete range of supplies services. In addition to a national headquarters, six operating divisions have been set up regionally, each covering between 40 and 50 major hospitals and all other NHS units within their area. (See Figures 14.1 & 14.2.) NHS trusts are not obliged to use NHSSA services, but if they were to source their supplies independently, they would not be able to gain access to NHSSA divisional or national contracts.

Purchasing in the NHS is being organized so that there are only three levels of activity:

- Unit level (a hospital)
- Divisional level (the six divisions described above)
- National level

It is envisaged that most purchasing will take place at divisional level. However, when the National Purchasing Unit establishes national contracts, they will be mandatory on divisional and unit-based supplies staff.

At the time of writing (March 1992) the NHSSA is at an early stage of its existence. Most key appointments have been made, but much work remains to be done in evolving strategies and policies. The effects on the supplier base could be considerable. It is obviously in the interests of companies and trade associations involved with NHS supplies business to maintain a close dialogue with the authority during the formative early phases.

15
Overseas Development Administration

The ODA, part of the Foreign and Commonwealth Office, is responsible for Britain's aid programme to developing countries (£1.8 bn in 1989). This programme helps generally to build up future markets for British goods and services but, more specifically, currently finances such business, either directly through bilateral aid or indirectly through multilateral aid.

BILATERAL AID

This accounts for about 60 per cent of total British aid and mainly goes to Commonwealth countries. It is generally tied to the procurement of British goods and services. Each recipient country is allocated a certain sum, within which it originates project proposals. Thus the initiative rests with the recipient government. It is therefore important for British companies to establish that projects of interest to them have sufficiently high priority in the recipient country's plans so that aid finance is requested.

Once projects have been proposed by the recipient country they are appraised and approved by the ODA, but then the actual procurement of goods is handled by specialist procurement agencies such as the Crown Suppliers.

Aid and Trade Provision (ATP)
This is a separate allocation of funds within the bilateral programme. ATP funds are intended to support projects of particular commercial and industrial importance to Britain, though not for business which could reasonably be expected to be won on normal commercial terms. It is

particularly intended to enable the UK to be competitive with the aid terms offered by other countries. The very significant procedural difference compared to non–ATP bilateral aid is that the initiative in seeking ATP support lies with the British company concerned, and its approach is made initially through the DTI, which appraises the request in terms of its significance for the UK industrial base. Thereafter the ODA conducts its own evaluation and the final approval is given by its Minister of Overseas Development, who is responsible to Parliament for the Aid Budget.

MULTILATERAL AID

This accounts for about 40 per cent of total British aid, with nearly half going to EC programmes. Other organizations in which Britain participates are the World Bank, the UN Agencies and the Regional Development Banks.

Multilateral aid is not tied, and British firms can tender for the contracts put out by the aid agencies. Under agreed procedures, invitations to bid have to be advertised in the press of the recipient country, and the local British diplomatic mission has to be informed.

MAKING CONTACT

Businesses must have access to information on upcoming prospects under these programmes, and need advice on coping with the detailed procedures and documentation involved. Both the ODA and the DTI are fully geared up to help, and publish numerous bulletins and guidance notes. These two booklets, in particular, provide full contact lists: *British Overseas Aid: Opportunities for Business* ODA 1991, *The Aid and Trade Provision: Guidelines for Applicants* DTI 1988.

16
Foreign and
Commonwealth
Office

The most direct impact of the FCO on the business community is the commercial work done abroad by the diplomatic service to encourage British exports. This work accounts for around one-third of the manpower deployed in British embassies, high commissions and consulates. The Whitehall mechanism for tapping into this extensive network of knowledge of overseas markets is Overseas Trade Services, the brand name of a joint directorate of the FCO and DTI, which was established in April 1991, drawing on units previously separately housed in the two departments.

Overseas Trade Services can call upon some 2,000 staff worldwide concerned with assisting British exporters, based in DTI London, the regional DTI offices and 185 diplomatic posts overseas. It works closely with the export promotion functions of the Scottish, Welsh and Northern Ireland offices. Some of the help provided by Overseas Trade Services is based on work done purely in the UK, whether by UK DTI staff, or through schemes managed by the Association of British Chambers of Commerce, etc. Some examples of the services provided by FCO staff abroad, though accessed through UK DTI offices, are detailed below:

Market Information Enquiry Service
Once you have identified an overseas market for your product or service which you would like to investigate in more detail, this service arranges for staff in the relevant diplomatic service post to complete a report, containing some or all of the following aspects:
- General background, political and economic information
- Brief general description of the relevant industry

- Details of the specific market for the product or service
- An assessment of your market prospects
- Recommendations on future activity
- Lists of agents, buyers and distributors
- Business reports
- Tariff information
- Information on relevant legislation

Export Representative Service

When you have reached the point of contemplating the appointment of an overseas agent or distributor, this service provides recommended candidates, not merely lists. The diplomatic service staff conduct an investigation drawing on their local knowledge and contacts, and undertake detailed discussions with potential representatives. You are then provided with a report containing a shortlist of agents or distributors who have been checked and recommended by the staff and who have expressed an interest in your product.

The report will contain advice on your recommended representatives, including their trading interests, capabilities, scope of activities, territory they can cover, warehousing and distribution facilities, salesforce, technical know-how, after-sales support, and other agencies held, but will not include a credit rating, which is best obtained through a bank.

New Products from Britain Service

This service aims to secure coverage of your product or service in appropriate publications in your chosen overseas market. Based on your publicity material and on telephone interviews, a journalist appointed by the Central Office of Information produces a professional press release, which is translated and then placed – subject to editorial discretion – by diplomatic service staff in suitable publications in the market concerned.

These and other services are charged for, though at very modest rates e.g.; for up to four hours work at the overseas post, £65 including VAT. Details on all the services, together with descriptive booklets, are available from DTI Offices (see Appendix D).

17
The National Economic Development Council

The NEDC, and its supporting organization, the National Economic Development Office (NEDO) embrace interests outside Whitehall. The Council (see Figure 17.1) consists of six Cabinet Ministers; six trade union general secretaries, including the General Secretary of the TUC; six representatives of the CBI, including its President and Director-General; the Governor of the Bank of England; and a number of independent members, including one with a consumer background. NEDC members (and the NEDO Director-General) are appointed by the Chancellor of the Exchequer, who normally chairs its quarterly meetings though the Secretary of State for Employment and for Trade and Industry sometimes do so.

Founded, (by a Conservative Government) in 1962, the task of the NEDC is to examine and improve national economic performance. Its special feature is to approach that task within a tri-partite (or multi-partite) structure. During the Thatcher era it was another institution of the old order which was marginalized, but nonetheless survived the cull of numerous quangos. It now has a long, continuous – and probably unique – history as a forum where government, business, the unions and others regularly sit down and discuss analysis of, and prescriptions for, economic and industrial problems.

The work is organized through 18 sector groups and working parties (also tri-partite) concerning different parts of industry or particular issues, some cutting across sectors. These groups therefore bring together some 80 senior business executives, trade union officials, civil servants and others, looking at concrete industrial and economic problems. Neither a lobby nor a pressure group, this unpaid and largely unsung network does provide a mechanism for communicating across the institutional barriers. Its success

Figure 17.1 The National Economic Development Council
(as at May 1991)

The Rt. Hon. Norman Lamont MP, Chancellor of the Exchequer
Chairman
Sir James Ackers, President of the Association of British Chambers of Commerce
Mr John Banham, Director-General of the Confederation of British Industry
Mr Rodney Bickerstaffe, General Secretary of the National Union of Public Employees
The Rt. Hon. Kenneth Clarke QC MP, Secretary of State for Education and Science
Sir Brian Corby, President of the Confederation of British Industry
Ms Brenda Dean, General Secretary of the Society of Graphical and Allied Trades
Mr John Edmonds, General Secretary of the General, Municipal, Boilermakers and Allied Trades Unions
Dr Walter Eltis, Director-General of the National Economic Development Office
Mr Eric Hammond OBE, General Secretary of the Electrical, Electronic, Telecommunications and Plumbing Union
The Rt. Hon. Michael Heseltine MP, Secretary of State for the Environment
The Rt. Hon. Michael Howard QC MP, Secretary of State for Employment
Mr Bill Jordan, President of the Amalgamated Engineering Union
The Rt. Hon. Robin Leigh-Pemberton, Governor of the Bank of England
The Rt. Hon. Peter Lilley MP, Secretary of State for Trade and Industry
Professor Roland Smith, Chairman of British Aerospace plc
Sir Bryan Nicholson, Chairman of the Post Office
Mr Tom O'Connor, Chairman and Managing Director ELTA Plastics Ltd
Mr George Younger, Chairman of the Royal Bank of Scotland
Sir Allen Sheppard, Chairman and Chief Executive of Grand Metropoilitan plc
Mr Ron Todd, General Secretary of the Transport & General Workers Union
The Rt. Hon. John Wakeham MP FCA JP, Secretary of State for Energy
Dame Rachel Waterhouse, former Chairman of Consumers' Associations' Council
Mr Norman Willis, General Secretary of the Trades Union Congress
Sir Brian Wolfson, Chairman of Wembley Stadium Ltd

depends on the goodwill of the participants, especially government; and on the quality of the research and policy work.

In addition to the interactions between the parties involved in the various groups, NEDO also organizes policy seminars. These are off-the-record discussions of major policy issues such as incentives for the low paid, reducing inequalities, and training and competitiveness. Papers written by NEDO staff or outside experts are presented to invited audiences of academics, civil servants, industrialists and trade unionists. These papers, and a summary of the policy conclusions, are normally published.

The Secretariat for NEDC and the sector groups and working parties is provided by NEDO's 110 strong staff, which is divided into Industrial, Economic and Management Divisions, supported by Communications Division and administrative staff. Work is also commissioned from outside consultants and experts; and ensuing activities, e.g., conferences and publications are often conducted in collaboration with others, e.g., DTI, or with the sponsorship of, e.g., Barclays Bank. Sector groups are constituted for a period of two years to examine and report on the performance of a specific industry. Working parties, with a lifespan of around 18 months, examine a specific aspect of industrial performance. The criterion for setting up or maintaining a sector group or working party is that any tri-partite committee should offer the realistic prospect of material improvement in economic performance. The Directors–General of NEDO and CBI, the General Secretary of the TUC and the Permanent Secretary to the Treasury meet twice a year to review the committee structure against that criterion.

Since the scope of NEDO covers such a wide variety of industries, all with their own market characteristics and problems, it is difficult to generalize about the work actually done. The case study set out below, however, gives a flavour of the sort of activity which takes place.

Specialized Organics Sector Group
The United Kingdom chemicals industry is one of the most successful parts of the British economy and in 1989 accounted for 6.3 per cent of manufacturing employment and a £2.1bn trade surplus. The principal companies are all multinationals, many of them British owned and based. The work of the National Economic Development Council sector groups and working parties is therefore concentrated upon those parts of the industry where there is a special need, such as the specialized organics sector, which is successful but characterized by relatively small, entrepreneurial specialist companies.

The sector group works mainly to improve the industry's world market share through improving its communications with customer sectors, especially in relation to the development of new products.

Co-ordinated programmes for the exploitation of the Japanese and US markets have been devised, involving the use of Inward and Outward Missions. This project is in partnership with the Chemicals Industry Association and the Department of Trade and Industry. A promotional leaflet has been produced aimed at potential customers overseas and at home.

A two-day workshop is organized annually. In 1990 the workshop addressed the problems and opportunities in the US market. In 1991 it concentrated on the development of the sector's business with Japan.

The sector group continues to work with SORIS, the Specialized Organics Information Service, which it founded and which fulfils a broking role in marrying United Kingdom companies able to take up a business opportunity by pooling their respective technical skills and combining items from their ranges of chemical products. The sector group also continues to support the Special Chemical Return which highlights market opportunities for United Kingdom specialized organics companies and which is now run on an independent basis.

The industry has a record of co-operation and collaboration among its constituent companies and the sector group has published a report identifying potential opportunities for collaborative research and development. A report has also been published following collaborative export market research on business opportunities in Finland and Sweden.

Work has been undertaken on the identification and assessment of opportunities for the sector arising from 1992. The group published a report in 1989 identifying some of the main directives affecting the industry and signposting advice and information

More recent initiatives have included surveys on incineration capacity and on the new business opportunities that will occur following changes in the competitive and regulatory environment. Environmental issues will form a major theme of the sector group's work over the next two years.

Part III

Lobbying Parliament

18
Introduction

As we have seen, Whitehall departments impact on business in many different ways and it is up to business to communicate with those departments directly on whatever concerns them. What then is the relevance of Members of Parliament, and of the various activities of Parliament? In what circumstances should business seek to communicate with Parliament, in what ways, and with what likely effect?

The general rule is that, where possible, it is best to seek to resolve the matter concerned with Whitehall departments and those bodies influencing Whitehall before adopting a parliamentary approach. There are several reasons for this.

First, and most fundamentally, it must always be remembered that in most matters relating to business, the executive, that is, Ministers and officials, normally holds the initiative over the Legislature (Parliament). Polices originate outside Parliament, consultations take place outside Parliament, even parliamentary Bills are drafted outside Parliament. It follows that, in general, when issues acquire a parliamentary dimension, events will have taken their course for some time before; attitudes will have hardened, lines will have been taken and deals done. This is not meant to imply that Parliament is a mere rubber stamp. It can never be taken for granted by Ministers, and in practice is not so regarded by them. As we will see later, important changes to government proposals can occur as part of the parliamentary process. However, this often arises as much from insufficient preparation or poor drafting in the pre-parliamentary stages, as from genuine changes of ministerial minds in the face of effective advocacy or pressure in Parliament. The typical treatment of a business issue in Parliament is low-key, with a well-researched and properly consulted piece of work by Whitehall emerging from Parliament in much the shape in which it entered.

Second, Whitehall has more time and more resources to consider any subject than does Parliament. Departments work a regular day, five days a week, all year. The House of Commons works outlandish and inefficient hours, on as few as 33 weeks in the year (1989/1990 session). Although Whitehall manpower has diminished considerably in recent years, Ministers still have considerable numbers of advisers and researchers at their service. Members of Parliament are, by comparison, very poorly equipped. It is only comparatively recently that all MPs have had a desk and a chair of their own, albeit squeezed into a room with several others, and often sharing a secretary. Full time personal researchers are rare, and part-time researchers are usually young and inexperienced (a significant number are American students), although all MPs have access to the much admired research staff of the House of Commons Library. Departmental Select Committees, the only mechanism available in Parliament for the systematic scrutiny of departments, have one House of Commons staff clerk and a part-time researcher to enable them to examine the purview and performance of an entire Whitehall department.

Not only are MPs ill-matched with a department's resources, they are also subject to a relentless barrage of lobbying from every conceivable direction, in a way which individual departments escape. The Department of Transport, say, is unlikely to be under pressure from anti-vivisectionists, anglers and the arts lobby, just to start with the first letter of the alphabet, but back bench MPs most certainly are, and from many others besides. Businesspeople must face the uncomfortable truth that many MPs will make the judgment that their political self-interest will be better served by attending more to the problems of the anglers than the businesspeople.

Third, as soon as a subject appears on the parliamentary agenda, it runs a risk, bordering on certainty, of becoming politicized. That is not to imply that until that point Whitehall considers subjects in terms of purest objectivity, unsullied by political considerations. Far from it; Ministers are politicians and both Ministers and officials know they have to get their measures through Parliament. But once actually within Parliament, the measures are likely to be exposed to a highly competitive and gladiatorial style of politics. This renders it imperative for Opposition spokesmen to fault the Government's treatment of any given subject and for the relevant Minister and his supporters to reply in kind, both sides drawing on such political ammunition as may be to hand (relevant or otherwise), and generally seeking to score points. There are always exceptions to this, and much though not all of the work of the departmental select committees is bi-partisan. However, it is generally true that, in Parliament, consideration of the objective characteristics of the matter concerned may always be inhibited by the need to respond to the political atmosphere of the day – or even the hour.

Despite all these reservations, there will come a time when the businesspeople will wish to address Parliament in some way, whether the issue of concern is on the parliamentary agenda or not. In this section we will discuss the subject under four broad headings:

- The role of the individual MP
- The formal business of Parliament
- Improving links between business and Parliament
- The regulation of parliamentary lobbyists

19
The Individual MP

CONSTITUENCY ASPECTS

All businesses will be corporate constituents of some MP, and many of the management and staff are likely to be his individual constituents. The MP will feel obliged, at the very least, to listen to a problem brought to him by a local businessman, even when the MP's political attitudes might not naturally be sympathetic. If they are, so much the better, and it will obviously be advantageous in having the problem dealt with by government if the MP belongs to the party in power.

The best procedure is to write to the MP at the House of Commons, requesting a meeting if necessary, but in any event attaching a concise statement of the problem (no more than two or three pages at this stage). This should be written in non-technical language, giving the background, the effect on the business and its employees, what needs to be done and what communication, if any, has taken place with government and with what result. The MP can then act in various ways, depending on the importance of the issue, his attitude to it, and the stage matters have reached. This could range from sending on the letter to the appropriate Minister, approaching him informally in the House, arranging a formal meeting with him in the department, intervening in the process of public legislation, if that is where the matter stands, or initiating legislation himself (see next chapter). A Minister will normally always agree to see a fellow MP, irrespective of party, on a constituency matter. Similarly, a letter from an MP will receive prompt attention in the department, as will a formal parliamentary question, which is published, and which must be answered orally or in writing, the reply also being published.

Parliamentary protocol dictates that usually an MP will only deal with his parliamentary colleague, the Minister, not with officials. If the outcome of your MP's intervention on your behalf is the offer of a meeting with officials to discuss the problem, your MP will not normally attend.

Businesses should consider developing a long term relationship with their constituency MP, as a source of informed political intelligence. It is obviously a matter of judgment as to whether the individual concerned is likely to be responsive and the chemistry of the relationship satisfactory. If the omens are favourable, contact should be established on a regular basis by arranging meetings and site visits on Fridays or during parliamentary vacations. The MP's personal political needs should not be forgotten; nor, of course, should they be slavishly pandered to. It would be acceptable and sensible, for example, to invite him from time to time to present awards to apprentices or open a new extension; in other words, to involve him in events which would be covered by the local press and thus provide him with some modest publicity not of his own initiation.

AN MP ON THE BOARD

Businesses frequently consider whether their links with government would be strengthened by appointing an MP to a non-executive Board position, or as a retained, paid adviser. Some MPs hold board positions or advisory roles because of a background in the industry concerned, or because of their professional skills in law, finance, etc., but we are here concerned with the merits of such appointments for their political qualifications. The ostensible advantages are of a dedicated link with Parliament, confidential advice, contacts, and, in the eyes of some, prestige. There are, however, significant disadvantages, particularly if it is thought that the MP will be able to represent the company's interests in Parliament and thus to government.

All MPs must register their interests, including directorships and consultancies, in *The Register of Members Interests'*, which is a public document. The member's affiliation will therefore be known to other Members, Ministers and officials. Indeed, it is customary, in addition, for MPs to declare their interest orally when making a contribution to a debate. It has to be said that, such is the chemistry of Westminster and Whitehall, the remarks of an MP on a subject related to an interested party to whom he is a paid adviser will be discounted. The depth of the discount will, of course, depend on the particular subject and how an MP handles the matter, but he will in some degree be tainted. Political opponents are likely to make an issue of his affiliation; and officials will be sure to remind Ministers of the association. MPs are far more likely to persuade their colleagues of the merits of an issue if they speak convincingly from a stand-point known to be independent. It is even more desirable for a company to have its case argued by an MP who is not only disinterested but is an acknowledged specialist in transport, taxation, etc. Many MPs do adopt special subjects without necessarily seeking consultancies. In fairness, some MPs who do accept outside appointments contend that this brings relevant experience to bear on the deliberations of the House; but this argument does not carry much weight in the cynical atmosphere of Parliament.

Information, links with Parliament, and contacts can all be supplied by government affairs consultants or 'lobbyists', who, whatever their merits and demerits, have no ethical problems in representing the interests of their clients. Their visibility, standards and accountability are under review, as will be discussed in Chapter 22.

THE HOUSE OF LORDS

Although the focus within Parliament is usually, and naturally, upon the House of Commons, the businessman should not ignore the House of Lords. Every government department has a Minister in the Lords who is open to questioning, as in the Commons – normally in a more courteous vein, but not infrequently sharp and persistent. The active members of the House of Lords constitute a repository of considerable experience – former Ministers and the most senior officials, distinguished scientists and industrialists, etc. It would be a recondite subject indeed which did not have an expert on it in the House of Lords.

All legislation has to pass through the Lords, where it may be amended and usually is (except that for taxation and public expenditure). The Government can be defeated in the Lords, and often is. The House of Lords recognizes the primacy of the Commons and is careful not to be too provocative, but nevertheless asserts its independent, revising role. Therefore a member of the Lords can be approached by a company to take up an issue, whether during the passage of legislation or more generally. There being no constituency interests, the approach would be based on a known interest of the Peer in the subject matter at issue. The House of Lords has no *Register of Members' Interests*, but Peers would be obliged to declare any relevant paid consultancy or any other financial interest before making an intervention. The advice of a parliamentary consultant should be sought in identifying the best individual.

20
The Formal Business
of Parliament

In this section we consider the basic features of formal parliamentary business, and how to participate in them. It is not intended to be a substantive guide to parliamentary procedures, which are complex. Suggestions for further reading on Parliament are made in Appendix A.

An issue can be said to be formally before Parliament in three ways:

1. As being the subject of legislation, i.e., a Bill or Order, embracing the topic, is at some stage in its progress through Parliament to enactment. The classic example is the Finance Bill, which puts into law the Chancellor's Budget Statement, normally containing tax provisions directly affecting business. There are also frequent instances of legislation, of EC or domestic origin, on particular industries, either setting up a completely new legal framework, e.g., the various Acts privatizing telecommunications, gas, electricity and water, and establishing law, e.g., issuing a regulation implementing the EC Directive on time-sharing.
2. As being the subject of a Debate, Motion or Question. Apart from debates which are part of the process of legislation, there are regular short debates, either on broad themes such as the state of manufacturing industry, or more particular issues such as pollution problems arising from one factory. The opportunities for such debates may arise from the publication of a Government White Paper (a broad statement of policy), about which a Minister will make a Statement, followed by a debate, or from the regular late night adjournment debates, when back-benchers may raise any topic (as a result of winning a ballot), to which a Minister will reply, and in various other ways.

The two most common ways for an MP to bring a matter formally in front of Parliament are to put down a motion or ask a question about it. In the former case the procedure is to put down on the Order Paper (the agenda for the day's business) a motion to be debated 'at an early day' to the effect that, for example, 'this House congratulates the Scotch Whisky industry on its export performance and regrets that the European Commission has proposed measures for the taxation of alcohol which would harm that industry's export prospects'. Such a motion, known as an Early Day Motion, or EDM, stands no chance of being debated on any day, early or late. Its purpose is to demonstrate a degree of concern to the Government. The strength of that concern may be gauged by how many MPs put down their signatures in support of the Motion.

An MP may initiate a Bill himself – a Private Members Bill – under certain conditions. These can only make progress with government support. Every year there is a well-publicized ballot for MPs to introduce a Bill on certain designated Fridays. The first 20 MPs have some chance of taking the Bill forward, with government help. Immediately the results of the ballot are known, the successful MPs are inundated by pressure groups inviting them to adopt their pet scheme. This is not the best way, in general, to advance a business issue, but there are exceptions. Seek specialist advice.

3. As being under investigation by a Select Committee. There are various types of Select Committee; those of relevance in the present context are either the departmental Select Committees, which 'shadow' each government department and review its area of work; or those which scrutinize EC legislation. Select Committees frequently examine subjects of direct relevance to business. Obviously the Select Committee on Trade and Industry has a focal position. Committees will often summon witnesses from business to give evidence on subjects as diverse as motor vehicle components, supermarket prices and plans for the Channel Tunnel.

PARTICIPATING IN THE FORMAL PROCESS

Legislation

By definition, if a subject is before Parliament with a view to it being enshrined in law, it is somewhat late to seek to influence the matter. But let us suppose that attempts have been made unsuccessfully during prior stages in the process; or, because of ignorance, the parliamentary stage is the only avenue open to make representations. What can be done?

A Government, with a working majority, which has brought forward legislation, is unlikely to yield meekly to representations from a company or trade association that the Bill is a bad idea, will harm the industry, etc., and should be withdrawn. Unless there is a glaring and vital technical mistake, and even then with reluctance, that will not happen. The most realistic objective is to seek to introduce some amendment to the Bill. How and when might this be done?

The normal sequence of a Bill through Parliament is:

- Formal First Reading; (no debate) and printing
- Second Reading; debate on the general principles of the Bill on the floor of the House. No amendment possible
- Committee stage; line-by-line discussion by a standing committee in a committee room. Main time for amendments
- Report and Third Reading stage; a debate 'reporting back' the committee proceedings to the whole House. Amendments possible
- Same procedure in House of Lords, with amendments possible at same stages
- Lords' amendments, if any, agreed in House of Commons
- Royal Assent

It will be seen that there are several opportunities for amendments, and in practice Bills are almost always amended. Most amendments are introduced by the Government because they have found, on inspection, that the original wording was imperfect in some way, was unclear or did not correctly reflect their objectives. The number of occasions when a Bill is amended because the Government accepts the arguments on points of substance made by the Opposition or an interest group via the opposition is not great, because of the loss of face involved. On the other hand, a company or trade association can and should go to the Government, in the first instance via the civil servant handling the Bill, and propose reasoned amendments. It will always be advantageous to demonstrate that the defect in the Bill affects a large number of companies, communities or interest groups.

The MPs serving on the standing committee examining the Bill line-by-line are obvious targets for briefing. However, this process should not commence until as many concessions as possible have been obtained from the Government privately, through bilateral discussions. When that point has been reached, and you are still not satisfied, the next stage is to contact a Member from the Government side on the Standing Committee to intercede with the Minister privately. If that does not work, the only remaining practical course is to brief the Opposition spokesman on the standing committee to put down and speak to an amendment.

Government MPs serving on standing committees considering Bills at Committee stage are silent; many of them attend to their correspondence during the sessions. They are there, controlled by their whips, to support their Minister seeing the Bill through. The Opposition MPs' amendment will most likely fail, for the reasons given before, but the Minister will at least have to give reasons for not accepting it, and he may be persuaded to give some concessions, short of changing the text of the Bill, about how the law may be applied. It is also at this stage that constituency MPs can be approached (especially if they are of the same party as the Government) to write to the Minister supporting the amendment. The strategy is to enable the Minister to appear to be magnanimous and flexible in responding to the representations made to him, and bring forward a suitable amendment himself, rather than be seen to be conceding under pressure that he had 'made a mistake'. Constituency MPs may also seek to intervene in debates, or put down questions.

Of course, from a company's or trade association point of view, it is more important in the end to get the legislation right than save a politician's face. It may be necessary, if the concessions are not readily forthcoming, to keep pushing at any opportunity, up to and including the House of Lords, to involve the press and generally mount a campaign. In these circumstances, specialist consultants' advice should be sought, both to provide tactical advice and to deploy additional resources. (See Chapter 28, Campaigning.)

Questions and Motions

Essentially, the purpose of using these devices is to smoke out a Minister who has not responded satisfactorily to a private approach. It must be stressed again that it can be counter-productive to adopt the public route first. It might work, but there is a risk of entrenching attitudes. At the very least, a Question put down will cause the Minister's department to examine the issue again.

A Member must obviously agree to put down a Question raising the concern of the company. He needs to be briefed, and to be convinced of the need at any rate to have the matter publicly addressed. He may opt to apply for an oral answer, (although he is rationed in these), in which case he will be entitled to ask a supplementary question when the Minister has completed his answer to the first question. The Member need not give notice of his supplementary, and thus the Minister's civil servants will examine all possibilities and brief him accordingly. That is the real merit of an oral question – it guarantees that the subject is not simply given a public airing, but that the department looks again at the original complaint. However, of the 50,000 questions tabled each year, only 2,500 are answered orally – due to time constraints – the balance receiving a written reply, with no opportunity for cross-questioning.

Similarly, a Member must agree to put down a Motion, i.e., a draft resolution of the House, the terms of which draw attention to the company's problem. In reality, the limited time of Parliament is carved up between government and opposition, and the opportunities for individual MPs to promote a debate are severely limited and highly prized. When they arise, they will be used for politically interesting subjects, and seldom to ventilate a company's problems.

Select Committees

Although the work of departmental Select Committees is not concerned with the day-to-day business of the departments they shadow, and they are therefore unsuitable to approach about immediate problems, they are interested in major policy issues which may be brought to their attention in various ways, not least through the experience of individual companies or trade associations. The way in is through the Clerk to the Committee – a Parliamentary official – and the approach should be couched in terms of wishing to submit evidence to the committee, either in respect of a current investigation they are conducting or as background information on a significant policy matter concerning the department they shadow. In the former case, officials of the company may be invited to attend the committee hearings in person to answer questions, but in all cases a written statement from the company about the subject concerned would be welcomed. Care needs to be taken with the form of words used in communicating with a Select Committee. Overt 'lobbying' would be inappropriate. Again, specialist advice should be sought from a government affairs consultant.

Parliamentary Lobbying case study: the CBI and the Statutory Sick Pay Act 1991

Background

Under an earlier Act, employers assumed responsibility for paying Statutory Sick Pay (SSP) to sick employees but were reimbursed by the Government. In this new Bill, it was proposed to reduce this reimbursement to 80 per cent, though off-setting some of that cost by reducing the employers' National Insurance contributions, and to enable the Secretary of State to vary the level of reimbursement by regulation, i.e., an order with the force of law but not requiring a new Act of Parliament. Such secondary or delegated legislation is increasingly common. All such orders are subject to Parliamentary scrutiny in principle, but in practice often receive little if any debate.

The main objections of employers to the SSP provisions were:

- The reduction of the reimbursement from 100 per cent to 80 per cent
- The proposed power of the Secretary of State to vary the level of reimbursement without new primary legislation
- The proposed ending of compensation for National Insurance contributions paid on Statutory Sick Pay

The timetable of the main lobbying elements

1. After the Queen's Speech routinely mentioned 'social security measures' the SSP Bill was presented on 8 November 1990. Individual MPs were briefed by the CBI before:
2. House of Commons Second Reading, 26 November 1990. Given other preoccupations (this was at the height of the Conservative leadership contest), there was little interest in the House. HMG conceded nothing, and was clearly in a hurry to get the measure through:
3. House of Commons Committee and Report Stages/Third Reading, 28 November 1990. Not only did the Committee Stage follow only two days after Second Reading, rather than the normal week or two, but the Committee, Report and Third Reading stages were pushed through on the same day. CBI briefed an MP to lay amendments, which failed.
4. CBI internal meetings took place (especially Council and Smaller Firms Council), 28 November – 4 December 1990. CBI Members showed strong opposition to the Bill. Subsequently a meeting with the Secretary of State was held, but no real progress was made.

5. Lords Second Reading, 11 December 1990. On 7 December 1990, CBI sent all working Peers a brief, outlining objections and suggesting that the Bill should be withdrawn. Cross-party opposition emerged, deploring the cost to firms during a recession and the lack of consultation with business on the part of the Government.
6. Lords Committee Stage, 14 January 1991. CBI briefed selected peers and proposed the following amendments to neutralise the cost to business of implementing the Bill:

   - raising reimbursement back up to 91 per cent
   - re-establishing 7 per cent compensation
   - deleting Secretary of State's power to vary level without reintroducing primary legislation

   The first and third of these amendments were won.
7. Lords Report Stage, 22 January 1991. CBI sent a brief to selected Peers, 18 January 1991, reinforcing arguments and advising HMG to retain the neutralizing amendments which had been passed. HMG introduced an amendment giving relief to some smaller firms (thereby recognizing the Bill's weakness) and the CBI amendments still stood.
8. Lords Third Reading, 28 January 1991. The smaller employers' concession was improved by Lords. HMG announced a new concession to smaller employers. The CBI co-ordinated a letter from nine employers' organizations to the Secretary of State pressing HMG to withdraw the Bill.
9. Commons Consideration of Lords' Amendments, 5 February 1991. CBI briefed all MPs advising that HMG should withdraw the Bill or at least accept the Lords' amendments in full, on the following grouds:

   - the cost to business of £100m at time of recession
   - the inequitable effects
   - the Bill had been rushed through Parliament
   - there was no good reason for the Bill and it was obviously unpopular

Voting in the Commons resulted in the Government's proposed cut in reimbursements to 80 per cent being restored, as well as the less generous government concession to smaller firms. Also HMG claimed this reimbursement was in effect a Finance Bill and barred the Lords from debating it. They did not reintroduce the power to vary the reimbursement level by Order.

10. Lord's consideration of Commons' amendment 7 February 1991. The Lords accepted the amendments but not without protest at further use of 'Commons privilege'. Royal Assent, 12 February 1991.
11. The CBI deplored this unnecessary cost to business.

Conclusion

This case study illustrates, firstly, the sort of unglamorous, unpublicized activity which organizations like the CBI must address, in an attempt to avoid or diminish an increase in business costs caused by government action; secondly, the power of government to push legislation through Parliament substantially in a form and at a pace of its choosing; and thirdly, the use that can be made by a determined business organization of parliamentary procedures, particularly the role of the House of Lords, to continue to press its case to government. A more overtly newsworthy issue, at a time when the media were less obsessed by an outstanding lead story, would have enabled a wider campaign to be sustained. As it was, did the CBI achieve anything? On the face of it, very little – a concession to smaller firms and the removal of the power to vary the reimbursement level by Order. However, in parliamentary terms, the latter is not unimportant. A government which has to resort to primary legislation, with all the stages that involves, will encounter one of the worst enemies parliamentary procedure presents to the executive – pressure on the parliamentary time-table. Time spent on new social security legislation means less available for the Home Office, Transport, etc., and so will not easily be granted by the Government's business managers. Another obstacle is put in the way of increasing business costs overnight.

21
Improving Links
Between Business
and Parliament

Businesspeople, or at any rate industrialists, have never formed a large proportion of Members of Parliament. Lawyers, journalists, teachers and similar professions predominate, with a sprinkling of investment bankers. There is an increasingly strong representation of professional politicians – those who have moved from being student or pressure group activists, or from local government, into national politics, without the taint of having worked in productive enterprise. Of course, some MPs are non-executive directors of companies, and several hold consultancies with companies, though both such activities are difficult for Labour MPs to espouse.

It is plainly in the interest of the business community that Members of Parliament – of all parties – should understand the realities and problems of business.

As has already been suggested, companies should seriously consider putting their relationships with their constituency MPs onto a regular footing.

Businesspeople should be aware that in addition to formal procedures of legislation, questions, select committee hearings etc., there is an active informal dimension to Parliament, aside from social life, which presents opportunities for business to have two-way communication with parliamentarians.

The two main relevant categories are back-bench party subject groups; and all-party groups. The first consist of groups of back-bench MPs (i.e. not holding any government or shadow spokesman position) within each of the parties with an interest in transport, agriculture, education, etc. Their purpose is to enable those MPs to brief themselves on the subject, meet their ministerial colleagues informally, and keep in touch with the world outside Parliament by hearing speakers on the subject, making visits, etc. Sometimes, these have links with outside trade associations or professional institutes which provide the secretariat finances a programme of visits, etc.

The means of approach in both cases is through the secretary of the group. Names of the groups and of office bearers are published quarterly in *Dod's Parliamentary Companion*, and lists are also available from the Public Information Office of the House of Commons (see Appendix A).

In addition, there is a well-established organization, supported by all parties, which seeks to improve understanding between the two sides – the Industry and Parliament Trust. It was formed in 1977, and its main function is to organize attachments for parliamentarians of all parties, including the European Parliament, and for House of Commons staff, with member companies of the Trust (currently 50). The attachments last for 25 days, usually spread over 12 to 18 months, and enable the MPs to gain a much more intimate appreciation of business life than can be gained through the occasional works visit or presentation. The Trust is non-partisan, non-profit making and is not a parliamentary lobby. Its President is the Speaker of the House of Commons (for details see Appendix E).

22
The Regulation of Parliamentary Lobbyists

The increasing involvement of government in business has produced, in response, a considerable growth in political and parliamentary consultancies. Although this has only added to what has always been a substantial presence at Westminster of lobbyists from non-business organizations – e.g., charities, trade unions and pressure groups – it has been the growth of lobbying firms which has attracted attention and some concern.

The House of Commons, in the shape of the Select Committee on Members' Interests, has studied this subject over many years and reported in 1969, 1974, 1985 and 1991. The last investigation, on which this chapter is based, was the most thorough in the series, taking evidence from commercial and non-commercial lobbyists, MPs and academics.

While recognizing the fundamental right of the electorate to lobby the elected, and acknowledging the contribution to informed debate which lobbying can make, the Select Committee was concerned to address the worries which had arisen about lobbying and whether and how the system might be brought under some control.

The type of abuse which had been identified in previous years centred round the use of their privileged access to the House by journalists and, more particularly, the staff of MPs, who work on a paid basis for outside interests. A person who is registered as the research assistant to an MP has a photopass which permits easy access to the House; he or she may obtain parliamentary papers quickly and easily without payment; and will also be in a position to book rooms for meals and functions (in the name of the Member). Although not essential for serious lobbying work, these are facilities which are obviously attractive to commercial operations. The evidence is that they became too attractive to a number of operators and were abused.

As a first step in controlling these activities, a register was established in which Members' staff holding passes are required to register any relevant gainful occupation other than that for which the pass was issued. In addition, steps were taken to enable a pass to be withdrawn where there was clear evidence that the individual was primarily engaged in lobbying activities. Members were also limited to three photopasses for their staff. As a result of this tightening up, the number of staff registered as being connected with outside consultancies has fallen in recent years from 50 to 20.

The most recent Select Committee investigation did not uncover any misdeeds, but did feel that the House of Commons had to be concerned about the standards of an industry which impinged so closely on Parliament as to affect its reputation. No qualifications are required to be a lobbyist, nor is there any recognized professional training. The competence of lobbyists therefore varies widely. There are no universally accepted standards of good practice, ethics or discipline, and no representative professional body to conduct a self-policing operation. The question therefore had to be faced anew as to whether Parliament itself should take the initiative by establishing an official register of lobbyists, as exists in other legislatures.

All the previous Select Committee investigations had come down on balance against a register, on practical grounds of difficulty of definition and enforcement, and fears of creating a spurious elite. The 1991 report, however, identified a shift in the balance of opinion and has recommended a register. It would fulfill three purposes:

- Transparency and public accountability, by listing both those who lobby and their clients, and making the register available to the public as well as Parliament
- The provision of an authoritative source of information for MPs on lobbyists, clients and staff
- Regulating the impact of lobbyists on the proper working of the House, and avoiding the abuse of facilities provided for Members.

The practical problems of implementation have not disappeared, but were felt by the Committee to be outweighed by consideration of openness. The Committee visited Canada in 1990 to study the operation of a register system established in 1989, and concluded that, on the whole, it was working satisfactorily.

The recommendation is for a mandatory register, administered by the House of Commons, for 'professional' lobbying firms, i.e., excluding for the time being charities, pressure groups, trade unions, trade associations, etc. The way is left open for a statutory register to be developed when and if necessary. This would enable the purview to be extended to those who lobby government departments (as in the Canadian system); a register established by House of Commons resolution would apply only to the House (not to Whitehall nor the House of Lords). Similarly, the way is left open for the register to be extended to a non-professional one in due course. Lobbyists who did not register, or who provided incorrect or incomplete information could be held to be in contempt of the House, which is as effective a sanction as could be imagined for a parliamentary lobbyist.

The difficulty with the proposed scheme lies not so much in setting up a register but in ensuring acceptable standards of behaviour on the part of registrants. A code of conduct can be written, but how is it to be effectively policed? The Select Committee suggests a Professional Practices Committee drawn from the industry, but this seems open to the original criticisms about the nature of the industry. How would the credentials of members of such a Professional Practices Committee be established? On what defensible representative basis would they be appointed? These and many other problems remain to be solved, but the prospects for a register of lobbyists seem stronger now than for many years.

Below are set out the draft proposed rules for a register, together with the accompanying code of conduct to which registrants would be required to subscribe, and a draft complaints and distribution procedure. These texts are intended to form the basis for further discussions, should the House decide in principle to create a register.

Draft register for professional lobbyists

Scope and interpretation

1. This register and the associated Code of Conduct and draft complaints and arbitration procedure applies to professional lobbyists. Accordingly, any company (or partnership, or an individual person) engaged in parliamentary or public affairs consultancy, or work of a similar kind, and which lobbies Members of Parliament (or their staff) for reward on behalf of clients or which provides information or advisory services to clients to assist them to lobby on their own behalf shall place

an entry upon a register which shall be kept in the Registry of Members' Interests.

2. For the purposes of the register 'lobbying' consists of representations made to any Member of Parliament or to any member of his or her staff on any aspect of Government policy, or on any measure implementing that policy, such as contracts, appointments, loans or grants, or planning decisions, or any item of legislation, or any matter being considered, or which is likely to be considered, by the House of Commons or any committee of the House.

Arrangements for registration

1. It shall be the duty of the Registrar of Members' Interests to maintain the register in such form as shall be decided, from time to time, by the appropriate Select Committee of the House ('the appropriate Select Committee').

2. The arrangements for the public inspection of the register shall be similar to those made for the inspection of the Register of Members' Interests.

3. A copy of the register, as amended from time to time, shall be placed in the library for the use of Members. A further copy shall be available for public inspection.

4. The Registrar shall cause the register to be published quarterly and, prior to publication, every person or firm entered upon the register shall notify the Registrar in writing of any change, or shall confirm in writing that there is no change, in the entry.

5. Subject to the requirements made in later provisions, the exact form in which any entry in the register is made shall be determined by the Registrar. The Registrar may consult the appropriate Select Committee at any time on any matter relating to the form and content of the register, including the removal of all or part of an entry.

6. The Registrar may remove all or part of an entry at any time, and shall inform the appropriate Select Commitee accordingly.

7. Registration shall not give the right to any preferential access to the House or any services or facilities of the House, or to parliamentary papers.

8. It shall be the duty of all those who register to ensure that their entries are clear and accurate and are kept up to date.

9. Eligibility for registration shall be determined in the first instance by the Registrar, subject to any final decision, on appeal or otherwise, by the appropriate Select Committee.

Rules

1. Subject to the discretion of the Registrar and of the appropriate Select Commitee as to the form in which an entry is made in the register; any entry in the register shall contain the following information:
   (a) Full name and business address (or addresses).
   (b) In the case of a company, whether the company is public or private; the name (when relevant) of any parent company; the names of any associated or subsidiary companies and the names of all directors.
   (c) The names of all clients held during the previous year, identifying:
      (i) those clients to whom a lobbying service has been provided.
      (ii) in any case where the client is not the ultimate beneficiary of any service provided, the name of such beneficiary.
   (d) In the case of a company or partnership; the name of any Member of Parliament with a pecuniary interest in, or receiving pecuniary benefit from, the company or partnership (not being a shareholding purchased in the normal way).
   (e) The names of all those persons who are carrying out, (or have carried out during the previous year) lobbying services for the company or firm, or for an associated company or partnership.

2. In the case of a company, the directors of that company, or in the case of a partnership, all partners, and in other cases the individual person or persons submitting the entry shall be responsible for the accuracy of the information that entry contains.

3. All those who register thereby bind themselves to observe a Code of Conduct and to obey any associated disciplinary procedure, both of which may be amended from time-to-time.

4. Registration does not imply approval by the appropriate select committee or by the House.

DRAFT CODE OF CONDUCT

Preamble: Scope of the Code

1. This Code of Conduct applies to all who register. Any firm or partnership one of whose directors or partners knowingly causes or permits a member (whether a full-time or part-time member) of its staff to act in a manner inconsistent with this Code is party to such an action and shall itself be deemed to be in breach of it. Any member of staff of a company or partnership, as the case may be, who acts in a manner inconsistent with this Code must be disciplined by the employer.

2. This Code is intended to co-exist with other professional Codes of Conduct to which signatories to the register already subscribe. However, in the event of any conflict arising, or appearing to arise, the obligations of the Register, this Code of Conduct, and the related disciplinary procedure are paramount.
3. All those who register have the positive duty to observe the highest professional standards, particularly in their dealings with Members of Parliament; with Members' staff, with public servants, with fellow professionals and with clients.
4. All those who register shall uphold this Code and co-operate with Parliament and with other signatories of the Register in exercising vigilance in order to ensure the maintenance and enforcement of the Code.

General Conduct
5. All those who register shall:
   (a) Comply at all times with the rules relating to the register;
   (b) Conduct their professional activities in accordance with the public interest;
   (c) Have a positive duty to respect the truth;
   (d) Not disseminate false or misleading information knowingly or recklessly; and shall exercise proper care to avoid doing so inadvertently;
   (e) Ensure that the actual interest of any organization with which it may be professionally concerned is fully declared;
   (f) When working in association with other professional persons, identify and respect the Codes of those professions;
   (g) Honour confidences given in the course of professional activity;
   (h) Avoid any professional conflict of interest;
   (i) Neither propose nor undertake any action which would constitute an improper influence on the organs of government or legislation or on the media of communication;
   (j) Neither offer, nor give, nor cause a client or an associate to offer or give, any inducement to any Member of Parliament, or any other person holding public office, or any public servant, or any member of any statutory body or organization, with intent to further the interest of any client (except that a director, executive or retained consultant of any firm shall be entitled to receive proper remuneration);
   (k) Not receive any commission from a client which involves any

element of payment by result (i.e., 'contingency payments'; or 'success fees').

6. No person to whom this Code applies may indicate directly or indirectly to a client; to a prospective client, or otherwise, that entry to the Register in any way constitutes approval by Parliament. However, it shall be permitted to draw the attention of any person whatsoever to the commitments that have been entered into by every signatory of the Register, in particular to the terms of this Code.

Conduct towards Members of Parliament

7. Any person to whom this Code applies shall have the duty:
    (i) To inform any Member of Parliament who is approached on behalf of a client of the name of the client, the reason for the approach, and the name of the company or partnership employing that person.
    (ii) To inform any Member of Parliament, or any member of his or her staff, or any member of the staff of the House of Commons, from whom information is sought relating to any proceeding of Parliament of the reasons for seeking that information.
    (iii) While within the precincts of the House, to conduct themselves fully in accordance with the rules laid down by the authorities of the House.

8. Any person to whom this Code applies, and who is in possession of a House of Commons access pass in any other capacity than as a Member of the House, or as a Member of the House of Lords, shall not use any facility of the House of Commons to which that person has access in order to make any representations or otherwise to assist clients (either his or her own clients or the clients of his or her employer).

Conduct towards clients

9. All those who register shall:
    (a) Safeguard the confidence of both present and former clients and shall not disclose or use these confidences to the disadvantage or prejudice of such clients or the financial advantage of the member firm unless the client has released such information for public use, or has given specific permission for its disclosure; except upon the order of a court of law or of the House of Commons.
    (b) Inform a client of any shareholding or financial interest held by that firm or by any member of that firm in any company, firm or person whose services it recommends.

(c) Inform a client of any fees, commissions, or any other valuable considerations offered by any persons other than the client; which are relevant in any way to the interests of that client.

(d) In no way misuse any information regarding a client's business or any other 'inside information' for financial or other gain.

(e) In no circumstances represent conflicting or competing interests without the specific consent of the clients concerned.

(f) In no circumstances guarantee the achievement of results which are beyond the practicable possibility of achievement.

Conduct towards other signatories of the Register

10. All those who register shall:

(i) Adhere to the highest standards of accuracy and truth, avoiding extravagant claim or unfair comparisons.

(ii) Refrain from any comment or action which would be liable to injure the professional reputation of others in the profession.

[There is an addition a Draft Complaints and Arbitration Procedure]

Select Committee on Members' Interests: Third Report 'Parliamentary Lobbying'. (HMSO)

Part IV

The Pressure Groups

23
The Business Lobby

The business lobby in Britain consists of individual companies and of organizations. To a greater or lesser degree, the top 50 or so companies will be in regular contact with Whitehall and Westminster for other than day-to-day commercial matters. Many have created an internal appointment (e.g., Manager of Government Relations) or, in the biggest companies, a whole department, plus representation in Brussels, whose responsibility, often with the help of consultants, is to monitor and report on political and governmental developments, organize regular contacts and conduct lobbying operations.

These companies make sure that their senior executives meet Ministers, back-benchers, and officials. They attend party conferences, provide and accept secondees to and from Whitehall, and are members of all the network organizations like the Industry and Parliament Trust or the Whitehall and Industry Group. The same names recur again and again (BP, ICI, IBM Marks and Spencer, etc.). Plainly, such companies know how to communicate with Whitehall and will always receive a hearing. It does not follow, however, that they are incapable of mistakes; or that Whitehall will accept their line without further enquiry. It is built into the Whitehall approach that organizations representative of the many must be consulted too, to ensure as wide a base as possible both for the grounds of any policy initiative, and for its defence politically.

The organized voice of the business lobby splits roughly into four:

● The Confederation of British Industry (CBI), speaking for the business sector as a whole
● The Institute of Directors (IOD), representing individual company directors

- The 110 chambers of commerce, around 100 of which are affiliated to the Association of British Chambers of Commerce (ABCC) representing small businesses (there are also some smaller business lobby groups representing, e.g., the self-employed)
- Some 3,500 trade associations and around 300 employers' organizations, representing companies in particular sectors. Many trade associations and employers' organizations are, in turn, members of the CBI

CBI

The CBI is the largest business organization in Britain, representing directly or indirectly some 250,000 businesses in all sectors, which employ half of the national work force. It is organized both regionally and functionally. All members belong to one of 13 regions, each with an elected regional council serviced by a regional director and staff. Members throughout the country have, therefore, the opportunity to debate issues of the day and have their views transmitted to government via the national council. Functionally, 16 standing committees consider subjects like taxation, energy, transport etc., and there is a variety of panels and working parties covering a myriad of topics.

Though much of the work of the CBI is concerned with providing services to members, its principal task is representational. To this end, its 300 staff include specialists in economics, industrial relations, law and technology, etc., and there is a Brussels office to facilitate communications with EC institutions. There is seldom any government initiative concerning business which is not made subject to some form of consultation with the CBI. Equally, there is seldom any concern of the business community which is not caught somewhere in the CBI network and transmitted in some form to government. The key to this two-way process is a patchwork of committees and panels. The CBI provides business members on the following UK organizations:

- National Economic Development Council (NEDC)
- British Overseas Trade Board (BOTB)
- Advisory, Conciliation and Arbitration Service (ACAS)
- Health and Safety Commission (HSC)
- Commission for Racial Equality (CRE)
- Equal Opportunities Commission (EOC)

In addition, the CBI represents the views of British business on various international bodies, including:

- Union of Industrial Employers' Confederation of Europe (UNICE)
- The International Labour Organization (ILO)
- The Business and Industry Advisory Committee of OECD (BIAC)

In total, the CBI Annual Report lists 122 committees, panels and working groups upon which CBI provides the business representation.

The CBI occupies a special position. Subsuming all sizes and types of business, embracing manufacturing and services, public and private sector, and including in its membership most major trade associations, it can sometimes sound like a government in exile. There are few subjects that a daring CBI President or Director-General would not feel able to pronounce on; and it would certainly be unusual if they failed to attract headline attention for their views on the economic, industrial and employment issues of the day.

In addition to its national presence, the CBI is regarded as the principal voice of business in the regions. This arises from regular, professional briefing of the media and through a 'parliamentary link-man scheme', of constituency MPs.

For much of the Thatcher era, some Ministers, at any rate, lumped the CBI together ideologically with other deemed excrescences of the old, failed, corporate state. This meant that, for some years, there was scant political recognition of the organization's authority and credibility. Down in the engine room, of course, there was no halt in the normal process of consultation on detailed aspects of policy and regulation across the board. Nevertheless, conspicuous attention was paid by the Government to the views of the Institute of Directors and other bodies held to be representative of individual entrepreneurs, despite their more modest research and consultative capability.

It took some years of jointly-shared experience, culminating in a second recession, for there to develop a more publicly constructive relationship between government and the CBI. Tensions persisted, however, and in the autumn of 1991 the CBI published an analytical critique of the role of the DTI and of government generally, produced by its Manufacturing Advisory Group.

Accepting that government should not intervene in the direction or management of companies, the CBI nonetheless argued that there was an important role for government in support of manufacturing industry in addition to providing the right climate, through anti-inflationary policies, investing in transport infrastructure, etc. The realities of international competition were that other nations gave greater support to their industries than did the UK. This reflected a more profound difference in attitudes and practices. Government and business in Germany and Japan appeared to operate together to a common purpose. In France a close-knit elite circulated between the civil service, government, industry and finance. In the USA, every administration drew heavily from business in filling senior federal government posts. By contrast, the UK economic policy establishment was fragmented and the worlds of government, civil service and industry were very separate.

The CBI levelled specific criticisms at the UK government machine.

- The DTI was preoccupied with regulatory responsibilities and was ineffective in promoting the interests of manufacturing within Whitehall
- Government departments, in framing their policies, did not appear to take into account the implications for manufacturing competitiveness
- The National Economic Development Council (NEDC) and its Office (NEDO) were ineffective as a forum for addressing issues of concern to manufacturing
- There was insufficient depth of understanding of the supply side of the economy within the Treasury and the Bank of England

The CBI recommended that the DTI 'refocused,' playing a lesser role in regulation and a greater one in promoting the international competitiveness of British business. It should take from the Treasury responsibility for NEDO and for the economic development committees covering particular sectors, with a view to creating a single point of contact within government for trade associations and a focus for action on sectoral issues. DTI should monitor the inflationary impact of policy proposals from other departments and champion the 'partnership sourcing' philosophy throughout the public sector. Efforts should be redoubled to expand the number of senior staff seconded in both directions.

At the time of writing, it is too early to forecast whether a realignment such as proposed by the CBI will in fact take place. In the post-Thatcher era, however, and under the pressures for government to compete for mastery of the EC decision-making process, it now seems likely that a less 'fragmented' structure of communication between business and government must emerge.

INSTITUTE OF DIRECTORS

Members of the Institute of Directors (IOD) are members in their individual professional capacity, rather than representing their companies. The IOD therefore has a close interest in questions of corporate governance, the role and responsibilities of company directors, and in providing appropriate training to enable directors to function effectively. The Institute also provides extensive services to its members, particularly in its London headquarters, and maintains a national and international branch network.

Although founded in 1903, the representational role of the Institute *vis-a-vis* Government was for many years low key, particularly when compared with the CBI and the main trade associations, until the Thatcher era. Then its track record of never having been involved in ideologically suspect activities like participation in NEDC, combined with its enthusiastic espousal of Thatcherite principles, gave it a higher profile and a more favoured position.

Its general stance, as 'advocates for capitalism, the market economy and the enterprise culture' remains bolder and simpler amongst the members of the business lobby. Nonetheless, and despite having a smaller research staff compared to the CBI and the larger trade associations, it produces policy papers and makes representations in London and Brussels on the detail of tax, company and employment measures. A solid programme of political contacts and briefing is undertaken, and evidence submitted to parliamentary select committees.

CHAMBERS OF COMMERCE

There are about 110 chambers of commerce in the UK. They are major suppliers of business services, notably with regard to international trade. They are also the largest private sector provider of a range of government-sponsored and fee-earning training, and are active in local economic development schemes. The pace of growth in chamber activity has been considerable during the last ten years. Staffing has increased from 800 to 3,000, turnover from £5m to £70m, and membership from 50,000 to 90,000 businesses. However, the picture is patchy. Only seven chambers have more than 100 staff, while some have only a handful. The breadth of service offered to members varies between regions.

The chambers, under their umbrella organization, the Association of British Chambers of Commerce (ABCC), have adopted a development strategy to strengthen and upgrade their network into a consistent, quality-assured and comprehensive service agency for all businesses in the UK. The aim is to close the competitive gap which exists with several continental European countries, where the chambers have Public Law Status. This means that all businesses are required to be fee-paying members and the chambers have a statutory duty to provide business services to their members. Consequently the system is well-financed, acts as the principal focus for a range of business services and joint business/government activities and avoids the fragmented system in the UK. Public law status in the UK would require legislation, which is unlikely in advance of a widely-based consensus and restructuring amongst business representative organizations.

This development strategy may or may not produce some degree of official recognition leading to a sounder financial base; but there is certainly a good deal of government support for the improvement of the network. The DTI has supplied secondees to assist in the process of rationalization and upgrading. Ministers have made notably supportive remarks. It is, of course, in the Government's interest to have an effective programme delivery vehicle and partner at grass roots level. Chambers have historically been close partners with DTI in export services and promotion e.g., issuing Certificates of Origin, organizing trade missions and advising small and medium sized companies on how to break into exporting. In more recent years, chambers have co-operated with DTI's enterprise programmes and close links have been formed with the Department of Employment's training and enterprise initiatives. As the chamber network is strengthened, the representational role of chambers will likewise be enhanced. At present, though policy committees at local and national level exist, meetings take place with Ministers and officials, and Budget representations are made, it would be true to say that the chambers do not yet possess the policy clout of the CBI or of the major trade associations. But much progress has been made in a short period, and the whole representational framework of business is ripe for renewal and restructuring.

TRADE ASSOCIATIONS

Apart from the CBI, the most powerful voice of business, as far as Whitehall is concerned, is provided by the trade associations. These vary considerably in both size and competence, and generalizations about them are unwise.

At one extreme, the Engineering Employers Federation provides an example of an active, outward-looking leader of the business lobby. The summarized account of the 1990 calendar of principal representational meetings and responses (reproduced below by permission) gives a useful insight into how a trade association communicates with Whitehall and Westminster, at national and regional level, on a wide range of issues, domestic and European.

January

- Meeting with Sheffield Labour MPs
- Giles Radice MP to North of England Association
- Written submission to the Secretary of State for Social Security regarding the Social Security Bill 1990, provisions for inflation, protection of pensions and the proposed pensions ombudsman
- Department of Education and Science accepts EEF representations on GCE A and AS level examinations
- Reply received from the Minister of State at the Department of Employment to EEF submission expressing concern over International Labour Organization (ILO) nightwork proposals.

February

- Meeting with John Caines, Permanent Secretary, Department of Education and Science
- Meeting with Michael Partridge, Permanent Secretary, Department of Social Security
- Meeting with East Anglia Conservative MPs
- Meeting with Sir Peter Middleton, Permanent Secretary, HM Treasury
- Written submissions to the Secretaries of State for Trade and Industry and Employment regarding the proposed European Company Statute
- Written submissions to government ministers and the chairman of the Government Advisory Panel on Deregulation regarding attachment of earnings orders for non-payment of the Community Charge
- Letter to the Department of Education and Science commenting on the Draft Order for Technology in the National Curriculum
- Government accepts in the Social Security Bill the EEF views regarding pensions
- Sir Geoffrey Howe QC MP, Deputy Prime Minister, addresses EEF Biennial Dinner
- Letters to selected ministers and MPs on the Statutory Sick Pay (Rate of Payment) Regulations 1989

March

- Meeting with Sir Peter Gregson, Permanent Secretary, Department of Trade and Industry
- Meeting with Sir Geoffrey Holland, Permanent Secretary, Department of Employment
- Seminar for Association directors on lobbying
- Written submission to the Department of Education and Science on the inadequacy of the design and technology component of the National Curriculum
- The Leader of the Opposition and members of his front bench team start a series of regional visits involving the Associations. These included East Anglia, East Midlands, London, Mid-Anglian, Sheffield, South Lancashire, Western, West Midlands and Yorkshire and Humberside Associations
- Parliamentary Group for Engineering Development grants the EEF *ex-officio* membership of its executive committee
- Written submissions to the Secretaries of State for Trade and Industry and Employment regarding the draft fifth European directive on company law
- Response to the Department of Employment on the proposal for a European Company Statute
- Response to Industry Matters *Aim Higher* consultative document on higher education policy
- Response to the NCVQ on the extension of the National Vocational Qualification (NVQ) Framework above level IV

April

- John MacGregor MP, Secretary of State for Education and Science, meets the Chief Personnel Executives' Consultative Group and the Manpower and Training Policy Committee
- The Director-General and Tony Greenstreet give evidence to the House of Lords ad hoc sub-committee on the European Company Statute
- Commercial and Economic Committee and the Parliamentary Group for engineering development briefing meeting on the EEF Engineering Economic Trends report
- Written submission to the House of Lords Select Committee on Science and Technology sub-committee on innovation in manufacturing
- Statutory code of practice on trade union industrial balloting comes

into force, reflecting three years of EEF representation

- Letter to the Department of Employment supporting the Secretary of State over the need for regular reports on member states' records in implementing European legislation
- Comment to the CBI on the European Commission working paper related to the proposal for a directive on typical forms of work

May

- Patrick Nicholls MP, Parliamentary Secretary of State for Employment, to Sheffield Association
- Meeting with West Midlands Conservative MPs
- Meeting with East Midlands Conservative MPs
- Meeting with West Midlands Labour MPs
- Written submission to the Secretary of State for Employment regarding the European Commission's proposed action programme under the Social Charter

June

- Tony Blair MP, Shadow Secretary of State for Employment, is the guest at the CPECG Study Conference
- Meeing with Sir Terry Heiser, Permanent Secretary, Department of the Environment
- Henry McLeish MP meets the Manpower and Training Policy Committee
- Michael Howard QC MP, Secretary of State for Employment, meets the Management Board
- House of Lords industrial relations debate (briefing supplied to Lord Caldecote)
- House of Commons debate on export trade (briefing supplied to Lewis Stevens MP)
- Nicholas Ridley MP, Secretary of State for Trade and Industry, visits West Midlands Association
- Irvine Patrick MP visits Sheffield Association
- Written submission to the Secretary of State for Social Security stressing the need for a Government statement regarding equality of state pension ages
- Written submissions to the Secretary of State for Employment and the Minister of State at the Department of Trade and Industry on the amount of European social legislation

July

- Meeting with European Democratic Group MEPs and European Communities' Economic and Social Committee members
- Meeting with Sheffield Labour MPs
- Response to BTEC on whether LEA schools should be able to operate BTEC First Diploma courses
- Response to Department of Employment on the EP(C) Act 1978 – Review of Limits

August

- Letter to Tim Eggar MP, Department of Education and Science, on the four-term school year
- Comments to CBI on EC plans relating to access to training

September

- Meeting with Chancellor of the Exchequer and his chief officials at the Treasury
- Comments to CBI on the EC Commission's consultative document on the proposal for a Community Instrument on procedures of information and consultation of workers within European Scale Undertakings etc.
- Response to Department of Employment on consultative document on EC's draft directives on atypical work
- Joint submission with the Engineering Council to the Chancellor, and relevant MPs and Peers, on the need for change to individuals' continuing education and training expenses
- Response to Department of Employment on the reform of the Careers Service

October

- Study visit to the EC institutions in Brussels led by EEF President, David Lees
- Meeting with David Trippier MP, Minister of State for the Environment, on the Environmental Protection Bill
- Informal visit from Michael Howard QC MP, Secretary of State for Employment

- Margaret Beckett MP, Shadow Chief Secretary to the Treasury, visits East Midlands Association
- Meeting with West Midlands Conservative MPs
- Response to Department of the Environment on 'cost recovery' plans under the Environmental Protection Bill
- Preliminary comments to the CRE on revisions to its booklet *Why keep Ethnic Records? Questions and Answers*
- Response to the Lead Body consultations on training and development standards and qualifications
- Letter to Department of Employment on careers education and guidance
- Comments sent to CBI on the Department of Employment's consultative document on a draft directive concerning the protection at work of pregnant women or women who have recently given birth

November

- Meeting with Dr John Eatwell, Economic Adviser to the leader of the Opposition
- Tony Blair MP, Shadow Secretary of State for Employment, to East Midlands Association
- Meeting with West Midlands Labour MPs
- Meeting with Anthony Coombs MP on tax relief for individuals' continuing education and training, with other interested organizations
- Members of the MTPC meet Henry McLeish MP to discuss the Labour Party's training policy
- Letter to Patrick Thomson MP on Statutory Sick Pay Bill in support of CBI amendments
- Response to the Department of Employment on consultative document on a draft directive concerning the protection at work of pregnant women or women who have recently given birth
- Comments on ACAS draft revised code on time off for trade union duties

December

- Exhibition at the House of Commons on 'The Importance of Engineering to the National Economy' sponsored by Patrick Thomson MP
- Michael Fallon MP, Under-Secretary of State, Department of

Education and Science, meets Chief Personnel Executives Consultative
Group
- Budget submission to Chancellor, relevant government ministers,
  opposition spokesmen, permanent secretaries, select committees,
  House of Lords spokesmen and members of the Parliamentary Group
  for Engineering Development
- Oral and written evidence to House of Lords EC Sub-Committee on
  European Commission's working time proposals
- Letter to Secretary of State for Social Security, the Rt. Hon. Tony
  Newton MP, on Statutory Sick Pay Bill
- Comments on the Engineering Council's draft policy statement on a
  'National System for Continuing Education and Training – A
  Framework for action'
- Letter to the Council of Local Education Authorities on the subject of
  a four-term school year
- Response to the Department of Employment on consultative document
  on employment and training for people with disabilities

The CBI, and other leading trade associations, e.g., the Chemicals
Industry Association, can lay claim to be undertaking comparable vigorous
programmes of representation, backed up with solid research. There is then
a considerable falling away, particularly in the quality of the research
foundation, which is all-important to have any effect in Whitehall. Grand
dinners with Ministers as guests make no impact if the case is not properly
prepared. Even within the CBI and the main trade associations, impact on
government can be patchy, and not only for political reasons. The different
constituencies within the business community – or any sector thereof –
make the representational task difficult. Small companies suspect large
companies; manufacturers have a low opinion of bankers; importers have
different perspectives to exporters; as do domestic companies against
subsidiaries of foreign companies; and so on. In any trade association there
are always some dissatisfied members. Government departments can – on
some issues, some of the time – gain a blurred impression of the 'business
view', or a clear but unhelpful impression of conflicting views; or may have
to wait a long time for any view to emerge. Nevertheless, Whitehall will
always consult the main trade associations and it is therefore in every
company's interest to support its relevant body, and work to ensure it is
properly resourced and staffed.

24
Consumers

Apart from trade unions, one of the longest lived pressure groups impacting on business and representing the individual rather than the corporate interest is the consumer movement.

Although some of the structures were established in the immediate post war period, notably the Nationalized Industries Consumer Councils between 1946–48, it was not until the 1960s that a more broadly based movement appeared, and not until the 1970s that the machinery and policy of government became engaged with it.

The best known manifestation is Consumers' Association (CA). Modelled originally on the Consumers' Union of the USA (founded in the 1930s), CA was established in 1957, with some financial help from Consumers Union. From the first decade of its life it concentrated on providing – as it still does – tested, comparative information on consumer goods. Its campaigning and representational or lobbying role commenced in the mid-1960s and really took off in the 1970s.

This period also saw the appointment in 1972 of the first British Minister for Consumer Affairs (Sir Geoffrey Howe), who, inter alia, took through the Fair Trading Act 1973 which created the Office of Fair Trading. The Labour Government 1974–79 created the Department of Prices and Consumer Protection and, in 1975, the National Consumer Council, with a remit to represent the interests of consumers to other bodies, notably central government. Although the Department of Prices and Consumer Protection did not survive the Conservative Government elected in 1979, there has always been since a consumer affairs function in the Department of Trade and Industry. The National Consumer Council continued, financed by the DTI. The 1970s also saw the emergence of a European consumer movement, with the establishment of the Brussels office of the European Bureau of Consumer organizations (BEUC) in 1973.

During this decade some relevant landmarks in CA's activities were:

- 1971: The Unsolicited Goods and Services Act, the first successful Private Member's Bill supported by CA
- 1973: CA is commissioned by DTI to advise the government on the likely effects on UK consumers of EC policies
- 1978: The Unfair Contract Terms Act and the Consumer Safety Act, both backed by CA, becomes law
- 1978: Following pressure from CA and BEUC, the European Commission sets up a separate directorate-general for environmental and consumer protection

During the 1980s CA evolved into the second largest consumer organization in the world, with a powerful established position in the UK opinion-forming and decision-making machinery. Members of CA's Council, staff and membership now regularly represent the consumer interest on statutory and public bodies, such as the Securities and Investment Board.

Consumers' Association, NCC, the National Federation of Consumer Groups and other consumer organizations are in regular contact to avoid duplication of effort, or, more positively, to co-ordinate campaigns for maximum impact. Although CA does not always take the lead, its experience and resources make it the primary focus of consumer representation in Whitehall. This position has been achieved not least by CA's skills in media relations. For example, CA in 1989/90 had contracts to provide research, locations and interviewees for the consumer programmes on Channel 4, BBC and ITV, in the last instance including the provision of a full-time researcher.

The 'front line' lobbying activity of CA covers issues as diverse as:

- Opposing the Weights and Measures Amendment Bill 1990. (CA mentioned 21 times during a five-hour Commons debate)
- Giving evidence to the Monopolies and Mergers Commission in a particular case of a manufacturer refusing to supply a retailer on loss-leading grounds
- Putting pressure on MAFF about the performance of microwave ovens, and joining a Government working party on the subject
- Briefing MPs on the Multi-Fibre Agreement
- Co-operating with the National Federation of Women's Institutes in a lobby of the House of Commons opposing food irradiation

- Giving evidence to a Government committee on banking law, plus follow-up meetings with Treasury officials preparing the subsequent White Paper

Business has now no excuse for ignoring the influence of the consumer lobby. Well-financed, professional, with mastery of the media and powerful governmental and international networks, it frequently sets the agenda for government action across a wide range of business-related issues. Having thus become institutionalized, the very familiarity of a consumer campaign concerning business may seem less threatening than, say, some headline-grabbing initiative. That would be deceptive. An estate of the realm has long since come into existence.

25
Environmentalists

Before departing for a meeting of the Environmental Council in Brussels, the Minister of State in the Department of the Environment goes through the agenda with the representatives of the Council for the Protection of Rural England and Friends of the Earth. (The Green Alliance representative needs to spend little travelling time to attend, since its Director is a special adviser to the Secretary of State and has an office in the Department.) There could be no more eloquent testimony to the central consultative position enjoyed by environmental organizations. This is not to imply that they, and others consulted, are in any sense creatures of government. They are independent (though some accept modest government grants); and much of their commentary is critical of government. The point is that they are firmly part of the Whitehall network, and often their representations will directly affect the interests of business.

The Council for the Protection of Rural England (CPRE) has a Head Office staff of 24, 44 Branches and over 45,000 members. An experienced organization, its approach is best described in its own words: 'CPRE's distinctive and hard-hitting campaign style is based on solid research, problem-solving and persistent lobbying. That is why CPRE is listened to seriously by Government Ministers, MPs, industrialists, the academic world and the media'. (CPRE Fact Sheet July 1991)

Areas of CPRE's campaigning impacting on business include:

- Within energy policy, mandatory labelling of electrical appliances
- Within mineral extraction policy, revised planning guidance for the extractive industries and a significant reduction in the level of open-cast mining
- Within agricultural policy, the scrapping of the set-aside scheme and its replacement with encouragement for less intensive farming

- Within transport policy, the replacement of the 'highly damaging' roads programme with the development of public transport, traffic management and effective measures for controlling traffic demand

The CPRE can point to demonstrable success with Whitehall for its research-based approach. Its policy papers are often substantial in length and sometimes commissioned from independent external consultants, e.g., a report by the economic consultancy PIEDA which the CPRE believes led directly to a Treasury decision to end tax reliefs for commercial afforestation. Similarly, a CPRE Report plus 12 case studies into a planning loophole allowing housebuilding in the open countryside for bogus agricultural need, elicited the following reply from the Parliamentary Under Secretary at the Department of the Environment: 'The CPRE Report . . . will be studied very carefully within the Department. Officials have been asked . . . to ensure that we give clear signals . . . on the need for close scrutiny of planning applications . . . claimed to be justified on agricultural grounds' (CPRE Annual Report 1991).

Friends of the Earth (FOE) won the title 'Pressure Group of the Year' in 1990 in a poll conducted by the advertising industry magazine *Campaign*. It has demonstrated its ability to mobilize massive popular support for its campaigns, achieve the level of media coverage which public relations professionals in business can only dream about, and gain acceptability and influence in political and governmental circles. The number of supporters has grown explosively from 32,000 in 1988 to 200,000 in 1990. This has brought not only signficant financial resources (1990 income £6.1 million) but also the ability to deploy highly visible groups of citizens concerned about various issues, equipped not with banners but with scientific measuring equipment and evidence on air quality, radioactive contamination, etc. Further, FOE has been able to master the procedural hurdles which can inhibit less well-resourced groups, for example, making a formal complaint to the European Commission about the breach of legal European air quality standards in parts of the UK.

The impact on business of FOE's activities is considerable. In 1989, over 100 local FOE groups lobbied electrical retailers to introduce minimum energy efficiency standards for domestic appliances. In the same year, a campaign was mounted against the use of CFCs in the construction industry. A year later, a survey showed that two-thirds of the top 50 architects and half of the top 70 construction companies targeted by FOE had implemented bans of CFC-blown insulation. In March 1990 a campaign was also launched to avert the destruction of peat bogs by commercial mining. Local FOE groups visited garden centres to inform the public about the alternatives to peat and lobbied the AGM of Fisons, the UK's largest peat extraction company. The following month, the DTI Advisory Group on recycling recommended that the Government should consider restructuring trade in peat and later banning it as waste-derived products become available.

The CPRE, Friends of the Earth and other pressure groups regularly work together. For example, in March 1989, a week before amendments to the report stage of the Electricity Bill were due to be debated, MPs received a written briefing signed jointly by CPRE, FOE, Worldwide Fund for Nature and the Association for the Conservation of Energy. In 1990, FOE organized an alliance of five trade unions working in the nuclear industry to call for a reduction in radiation dose limits, and, two years previously, submitted a Memorandum jointly with Greenpeace to a House of Lords committee examining radioactive waste disposal policy. There are many such examples, not limited to other environmental organizations. Three fuel poverty groups joined with FOE in 1990, calling for public spending on the energy efficiency of the homes of low-income households.

In addition, environmental pressure groups have an effective international network and are able to draw quickly upon international experience to present an (apparently) comprehensive and well-researched case locally.

This brief account does not imply that environmental groups are always right and their arguments well-founded. Far from it; but what is relevant is their effectiveness as advocates and the wielders of considerable political clout. Judged purely on the basis of effective communications, media attention, coalition-building and government lobbying, they put business organizations in the shade. It may be that they are riding on the crest of a wave of popular support which will have its day and then decline.

There was a previous wave of environmentalism in the 1970s which appeared to go into decline. But the prudent businessman would do well to assume that serious concern for the environment is an idea whose time has come and which has been absorbed permanently into the posture of governments, whatever may be other political differences. Thus, we see the Environmental Protection Act passed, the regulatory agencies reorganized, and concepts such as 'BATNEEC' (Best Available Technology Not Entailing Excessive Costs) evolved as a practical criterion for firms subject to pollution control. The DTI sets up an Environmental Unit, and publishes environmental contacts for business within government; the DTI and DOE establish an Advisory Committee on Business and the Environment; and so on. The Whitehall machine converts the political imperatives into schemes that can be made to work.

The environmental groups have established themselves in a powerful position in this process from start to finish, and it would not be an exaggeration to say that they set the agenda. The conclusion for business must be: participate in the process; communicate uncomplainingly with the groups, or suffer the consequences.

Part V

Whitehall in Action

26
The Case of
Eco-Labelling

As we have seen, the process whereby Whitehall comes to evolve policies and take decisions affecting business is one in which many interests are consulted and represented. Although it is impossible to produce a case study which can be said to be entirely 'typical' of the rich variety of business/ government situations, the issue of eco-labelling well illustrates a number of the aspects involved.

Eco-labelling is a scheme whereby products have the opportunity of being labelled, according to officially agreed criteria and procedures, as being less damaging to the environment than alternatives. The purpose of such a scheme would be to respond to the well-attested and researched desire of consumers to be able to take environmental considerations into account when making everyday purchases.

It requires no great leap of the imagination to see that any such scheme would have a widespread impact on manufacturers, retailers, those involved in marketing, packaging, advertising and many others. Just such a scheme, on a European Community-wide basis, was decided upon by EC Ministers at the end of 1991, to take effect in time for the planned completion of the Single European Market at the end of 1992. How did the UK Government evolve and progress its policy on this issue, and who was consulted, or made representations, with what effect, along the way?

ORIGINS

In general terms, eco-labelling, at any rate in the UK, originated as a public policy issue out of the explosive growth in the environmental movements during the late 1980s. A survey of British environmental groups published in 1983 estimated their membership at between 2.5 and 3 million. (Lowe

& Goyder 1983). By 1990 another estimate put membership at 4.5 million, or eight per cent of the population (McCormick 1991). Even allowing for the somewhat disparate organizations which are often lumped together under the environmental heading, this represents a mass movement in any terms. The significance of its size and growth would not be lost on politicians, the media or, indeed civil servants working in the environmental area, part of whose job is to be alert to developments in society affecting their Ministers' responsibilities and interests.

Probably the seminal event which focused environmental concerns on to everyday supermarket purchases was the Friends of the Earth campaign against CFCs in aerosols in 1988. There had been earlier campaigns, for example against lead in petrol, but the CFC campaign was significant in that it evoked a response among manufacturers and retailers, with regard to other products. A rash of claims appeared, to the effect that the products concerned were 'ozone friendly', 'environmentally friendly' and so on. Thus the issue of the veracity and standards of environmental claims made at the point of sale of household products started to take potential shape. (In some other countries, the issue had taken concrete shape and had been responded to many years previously: for example, West Germany introduced its 'Blue Angel' labelling scheme in 1978. This and other examples would have been well known to the strong international networks of consumer and environmental organizations.)

In the UK, 1988 was the pivotal year, when the issue of government action to provide authoritative guidance on point-of-sale environmental claims crossed the line between possibility and desirability. An important catalyst was the runaway success in that year of the book *The Green Consumer Guide*, by John Elkington and Julia Hailes, which topped the best-seller lists for several weeks. This caused great media interest: conferences and seminars on the subject boomed; and several other publications followed, including a *Green Supermarket Guide*.

DRAMATIS PERSONAE

The relevant part of the story of eco-labelling took place between 1988 and 1991, and involved the following players:

- Whitehall
- Parliament
- Business
- Pressure Groups
- European Community

The following account will attempt to sketch the roles played by these players, and their interactions, not in any great detail, but sufficient to illustrate the procedures involved.

1988 – WHITEHALL STARTS WORK

In 1988, Whitehall started serious work on an official scheme for eco-labelling. Though obviously of great importance to business, such a scheme was seen in Whitehall to be primarily a matter of environmental policy, and therefore the lead department was the Department of the Environment rather than the DTI. However, because the DTI is responsible for consumer affairs; because a labelling scheme required consultation with manufacturers and retailers, and because the DTI would have to decide whether the Trades Descriptions Act should be amended to ensure it covered environmental claims, it was decided at the start that the two departments would work together in developing the proposal. It seems likely that the trigger for starting work was a regular 'round-up' meeting between DoE officials and Ministers, when the former would have drawn the attention of the latter to the growing interest in the subject, not least on the part of the European Commission, and recommended that the Department work up some proposals.

Ministers and officials – who does what?

It is instructive to note the levels, both Ministerial and official, at which this subject is handled. The illustration below shows the relevant part of the departmental structures of DoE, with the grades of officials noted.

Within the DoE, basically all the work on eco-labelling was done by officials at grade 7 and grade 5 level, and the bulk of that by the grade 7 postholder. It was the latter, for example, who wrote all the documentation, drew up issues for discussion and decision, visited foreign countries to study their eco-labelling schemes etc. He did, of course, report to and consult with his senior colleagues up to grade 2 level through normal progress meetings and the circulation of drafts. Therefore the most senior officials would have an opportunity of commenting on or challenging the analysis and recommendations coming up; but the initiative in producing the latter rests very much with the grade 7/5 levels (the pattern was the same within the DTI). At certain points, more senior officials would lead for the Department, e.g., grade 3 when appearing before the Select Committee on the Environment (though the grade 7s were also present and spoke).

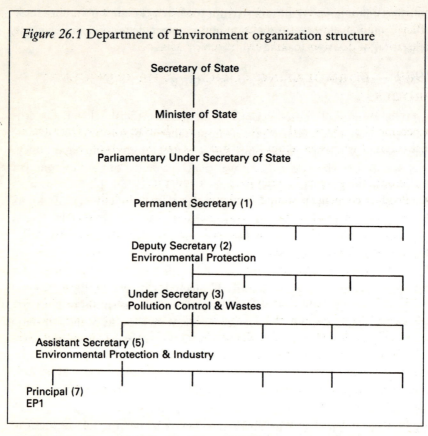

Figure 26.1 Department of Environment organization structure

Secretary of State

Minister of State

Parliamentary Under Secretary of State

Permanent Secretary (1)

Deputy Secretary (2)
Environmental Protection

Under Secretary (3)
Pollution Control & Wastes

Assistant Secretary (5)
Environmental Protection & Industry

Principal (7)
EP1

Ministerially, within the DoE, eco-labelling has been dealt with almost entirely by the Parliamentary Under Secretary. He is the Minister to whom most issues requiring a decision are put, though again, other Ministers are informed routinely. However a more senior Minister, with wider responsibilities, usually the Minister of State, represents the Government at EC Environmental Council meetings, where a broad agenda of issues is considered. When eco-labelling appears on that agenda, the Minister of State would take a brief and be accompanied by the grade 7 official responsible for eco-labelling. Also, it is conventional to announce many government decisions in the form of a written reply to a Parliamentary Question (the latter being engineered for the purpose). Such questions are normally addressed to the Secretary of State and the answer, usually with an accompanying press release, would be in the Secretary of State's name as was the case when the Government announced its decision on eco-labelling. It is up to every Secretary of State to decide how he will run his ministerial team, and with what degree of delegation. In this instance, official announcements notwithstanding, there has been the maximum delegation of decision-making to the junior Minister.

1989 – FORMULATING POLICY – THE CONSULTATIVE PROCESS

It became clear in the early work done on eco-labelling in the Department that certain basic issues about the scheme had to be resolved, e.g:

- Should the scheme be voluntary or mandatory?
- Product coverage – should food and drink be included?
- Criteria for environmental assessment of products – through their complete life cycle, or their impact in use, or their use plus disposal?
- Period of award of label?
- How to organize the scheme?

It had also become clear that the pressures for action registered in the UK were shared within the European Community. That immediately suggested the desirability of an EC-wide scheme, to avoid a proliferation of national schemes, which would run the risk of fragmenting the Single Market. Against that, the Departments were aware that a satisfactory EC scheme might take so long to evolve as to be politically unacceptable in the UK.

In this, as in all other instances where Whitehall is considering the details of an official scheme affecting the public, outside opinions are sought from those with relevant standpoints and experience. (An exception might be a candidate tax for an immediately forthcoming Budget). Although government departments and agencies build up expertise in areas both broad and specialised, they can never expect to have up-to-date and detailed knowledge of developments in, say, retailing. Even if they did, there are obvious political reasons to be seen to be consulting interests likely to be affected by the measures concerned.

The departments organized their consultations in two stages; the first, informal stage involved discussions with a relatively small number of people, drawn from consumer and environmental groups, retailers and manufacturers and with the European Commission. This enabled a provisional government view to emerge on the above issues. The second, conducted through the publication in August 1989 of a consultative discussion paper which stated the Government's provisional views, provided for a wider input and one more precisely focused on the matters which had to be resolved, both domestically and with the EC.

The discussion paper produced 94 public responses, listed in Exhibit 1. It is instructive to examine their composition:

trade associations, etc.	40
manufacturers and retailers	20
environmental groups	8
consultants	7
local government	6
consumer groups	3
individuals	2
educationalists	1
others, various	7
	94

No conclusions about quality and impact necessarily follow from the number of responses involved. In particular, the lead position of trade associations in the league table of respondents reflects the fissiparous nature of British business representation as much as anything else. The political clout of the environmental and consumer groups is independent of the number of their organizational responses. As previously noted, the number of individual adherents to those groups was not lost on government.

Further, the clarity and punch of a submission from an environmental or consumer group is normally far superior to that submitted by a trade association. The former are professional campaigners, who seldom submit the wording of a draft representation for approval to their membership; the latter are often constrained in precisely that respect, resulting in a bland formulation-seeking to reconcile the often conflicting interests of their membership in crucial matters of detail. This often robs trade associations of the colour and vivacity of language which earns column inches in the press, and thus political impact, though some trade associations have given a lead to their members on environmental matters. Reading the media coverage of eco-labelling, who would have thought that the bulk of thoughtful input came from trade and industrial organizations?

Between the two rounds of consultation, therefore, certain policy lines had been established, e.g., that food and drink should be excluded from the scheme, and that products would have to be assessed on their whole life cycle. Recommendations on these policy lines would have originated from the grade 7 official and cleared at 5 level and above, for ministerial decision by the Parliamentary Under Secretary. This is not untypical for a fairly straightforward piece of government policy-making. Eco-labelling was not a flagship Environment Department policy, did not have a high political profile, nor significant public expenditure implications, and did not arise out of a crisis. Other circumstances would have produced a different pattern of deployment of the official and ministerial machinery.

1989 – ENTER THE COMMISSION

Apart from the UK, other member states in the EC, such as Denmark, had been considering eco-labelling (West Germany have had such a scheme since 1978) and therefore the European Commission had been monitoring developments and evolving a view. The lead was taken by Directorate General XI (DGXI), responsible for the environment.

The first formal steps in the EC's procedure to produce a Community eco-labelling scheme was taken in September 1989, when the Environment Council of Ministers supported a proposal by the Commission for a scheme, the motivation being to prevent a rash of incompatible national schemes emerging.

DGXI then convened panels of experts (civil servants) from member countries to work on the details. This was to be the start of a protracted process within the EC which did not produce a draft regulation until February 1991. In broad outline, the procedure for evolving an EC instrument (whether directive or regulation) is for the proposal to circulate between the Commission, the Council of Ministers and the European Parliament until agreement is reached. The whole process can be dealt with in a few months if both Council and Parliament are in general agreement, otherwise it takes much longer. In this case, however, the delay was due to disagreement within the Commission bureaucracy itself as to the structure of an eco-labelling scheme, DGIII (Industry) favouring a more centralized and standards-oriented scheme than had emerged from the expert working groups led by DGXI.

1990: IN THE ENGINE ROOM OF POLICY-MAKING

As far as the British Government was concerned, 1990 commenced with an overtly crisp statement of purpose. On 9 January, the Secretary of State for the Environment stated 'We are committed to establishing a scheme that

161

is both credible and workable'. Presciently, he observed, with regard to the EC, 'We shall ensure that the organization involves a minimum of bureaucracy'.

He also announced that he and the Secretary of State for Trade and Industry proposed to set up an advisory group of experienced individuals to advise on the details of the scheme. However, it was not until May 1990 that the National Advisory Group on Eco-labelling (NAGEL) was established. Chaired by Sir Kenneth Durham, ex-Chairman of Unilever and Kingfisher, its membership is set out in Exhibit 2, and comprises individuals (not representing their organizations) from consumer groups, manufacturing, retailing, advertising and, a sign of the times, environmental consultancies.

This is an example of a frequently used Whitehall device. Advisory committees, panels and groups of varying degrees of permanence are to be found attached to most departments, a more institutionalized form of the consultative tendency we have already identified. They serve several purposes: to provide expert knowledge and external perspective; to recognize the importance of interest groups; and, not least in the present example, to increase Whitehall's capacity for progressing the detailed development of a policy initiative, whose success very much depends on getting the details right. Thus, soon after its establishment, NAGEL set up three sub-committees to work on how product groups should be chosen and the labelling criteria identified; how the scheme should be administered; and how the scheme should be promoted to consumers and manufacturers. Ministers do not attend NAGEL meetings, though they meet NAGEL members informally. The Group is attended and serviced by the grade 7s and their staff.

Similar detailed work, organized by DGXI, proceeded during 1991. For example, a number of member states were invited to lead pilot studies to examine how to establish the criteria against which particular product groups would be assessed in the process of being awarded an eco-label. The UK evaluated washing machines, the Danes paper products, the Germans detergents, etc. In these studies, the manufacturers of the products concerned were brought into what has, not surprisingly, turned out to be a complex task of carrying out life-cycle analysis of the environmental impact of very different products.

1991: YEAR OF DECISION

The European Commission published its formal proposal on eco-labelling, in the form of a draft regulation on 11 February. It differed greatly from the position the expert working groups had reached the previous summer, not in principles but in administrative structure and procedures. These were much more complex and centralized, involving for example a role for the as yet unestablished European Environment Agency (EEA) and for a central 'jury', comprising member states and other interests, which would decide which application for an eco-label best fulfilled the criteria, taking advice from the EEA.

The UK Minister of State, and Ministers from other member states expressed serious reservations about the proposed administrative structure at the Environment Council on 18 March. The proposed regulation was therefore referred to a council working group for further discussion. These officials were clear that the general political will existed for a Community-wide scheme, the danger of proliferating national schemes being evident. By December a compromise had been hammered out and agreed at the Environment Council in that month. Formal adoption was scheduled to follow by March and the scheme in use by the end of 1992.

Exhibit 1 **Respondents to environmental labelling paper**

Albright and Wilson Limited
Association of British Chambers of Commerce
Association of British Pharmaceutical Industry
Association of Makers of Soft Tissue Papers
Association of Metropolitan Authorities
Association of Sanitary Protection Manufacturers
Association for the Conservation of Energy
Barking and Dagenham Borough Council
Beecham Products
Boots Company PLC
Birmingham Chamber of Industry and Commerce
British Aerosol Manufacturers' Association
British Agrochemicals Association
British Association for Chemical Specialities
British Battery Manufacturers Association
British Ceramic Manufacturers Federation
British Gas
British Lawnmower Manufacturers' Federation
British Leather Confederation
British Man-Made Fibres Federation

British Plastics Federation
British Radio and Electronic Equipment Manufacturers' Association
British Retailers Association
British Scrap Federation
British Standards Institute
Bureau of Environmental Standards and Technology
Confederation of British Industry
Chemical Industries Association
Co-operative Union Limited
Conservation Papers Limited
Consumers' Association
Consumers in the EC Group (UK)
Cordage Manufacturers Institute
Cosmetic Toiletry and Perfumery Association Limited
Council for the Protection of Rural England
Countryside Commission
Coventry Pollution Prevention Panel
Cuprinol Limited
Cussens (UK) Limited
David Bellamy Associates Limited
Devon Conservation Forum
Ditchling Women's Institute
Electronics and Business Equipment Association
Federation of Wholesale and Industrial Distributors
Food and Drink Federation
Friends of the Earth
Hounslow Borough Council
Humberside County Council
Hydrotek Damproofing Limited
Incorporated Society of British Advertisers
Individual (Mr J. D. Carver)
Individual (Mr C. T. Meyrick)
Industry Council for Packaging and Environment
Institute of Trichologists
International Wool Secretariat
J. Bibby and Sons PLC
J. Sainsbury PLC
John Lewis Partnership
Kimberly-Clark Limited
LA Co-ordinating Body on Trading Standards

Lead Development Association
Lin Pac Plastics International Limited
Media Natura
Michael Peters Group PLC
Mills Associates Limited
Mothercare
National Consumer Council
National Society for Clean Air
Nucleus Design Limited
Oldham Metropolitan Borough Council
PA Consulting Group
Paintmakers Association of Great Britain
PIRA Packaging Division
Procter and Gamble Limited
Scottish Agricultural College
Small Electrical Appliance Marketing Association
Soap and Detergent Industry Association
Society of British Gas Industries
Society of British Match Manufacturers
Society of Motor Manufacturers and Traders
Soil Association
Sustainability
Tait Paper
Tesco
The Body Shop
The Environment Council
The Newspaper Society
Townswomen's Guilds (national body)
United Kingdom Petroleum Industry Association
WARMER Campaign
Worldwide Fund for Nature (UK)

In addition, responses were submitted by five individuals and bodies on a confidential basis.

Exhibit 2

NAGEL Membership

Sir Kenneth Durham, Chairman. Ex-chairman of Unilever PLC and Kingfisher PLC

Dr John Adsetts, Chairman, Product Categories Sub-Group. Albright and Wilson

Mr Kenneth Miles, Chairman, Communications Sub-Group. Incorporated Society of British Advertisers

Mr Richard Macrory, Chairman, Administration Sub-Group. Imperial College of Science, Technology and Medicine

Mr Ian Chalk, Reedpack Ltd

Mr Peter Green, County Trading Standards Officer for West Sussex County Council

Ms Julia Hailes, Sustainability Ltd

Ms Pippa Hyam, PDA International

Mr John Jack, IBM UK

Mrs Dorothy Mackenzie, Dragon International

Mr Steve Robinson, Chief Executive, The Environment Council

Mr Mike Rosen, Sainsburys

Dr Charles Suckling, Member of the Royal Commission on Environmental Pollution

Mr Nigel Whittaker, Kingfisher PLC

Lady Wilcox Chairman, National Consumers Council

27
Making Your Case
to Whitehall

Talking to Whitehall is much easier than might be supposed. Civil servants are, after all, public officials: part of their job is to listen to public opinion, and businesspeople, especially when employing many staff, form an important part of the public. More practically, officials will listen so as to get their department's policies right and keep their Ministers out of trouble. And, increasingly, officials will wish to be at least as well informed as their counterparts in EC governments and the Commission. Ministers share these motivations and, additionally, have the urge to be seen to be politically successful. Part of this often elusive achievement arises from being master of the situation, hence needing to be aware of all the interests affected by their decision-making.

Despite this potential receptiveness on the part of Whitehall, businesses often perform much more maladroitly in their communications with government than they would tolerate in their purely commercial operations. This is regrettable, since the observance of the following basic rules should minimize the difficulties.

TIMING

Communicate as early as possible, as soon as you have become aware of the problem or issue and have given it due deliberation. Whitehall is beset by timetables, whether imposed by Ministers, Parliament, the EC or the normal internal disciplines necessary for any organization to process its work. The longer you wait before making your point, the more likely it is that working parties will have been convened, consultations carried out, guidance from Ministers obtained and, in general, attitudes formed and options excluded, one of which might have been yours. It is difficult to change a department's policy once it has been enunciated in a White Paper, and particularly hard going if the matter has reached the legislative stage.

MONITORING

The oft-quoted advice to comment early in the decision-making process, while valid, is of course impossible to heed if you are unaware that the subject in which you are interested is being worked on. Therefore a prime requirement is to have some system in place to monitor relevant areas of activity.

Such systems fall into the following categories; each with their benefits and disadvantages, all requiring time and money.

An in-house appointment
A member of staff whose job is wholly or partially to act as the company's eyes and ears in Whitehall, by maintaining a network of contacts, serving on industry committees, reading relevant publications, etc. The main advantage of this approach is that the incumbent will presumably have a good grasp of the detailed implications for your business of any particular proposal. There can be drawbacks. Not everyone is suited to this sort of work. To be effective, the staff member needs to have something of a political 'nose', and he must be an effective communicator within the organization as well as within Whitehall. Not every company could justify the resources involved; and it is important, especially when economic times are hard, that everyone in the organization recognises the worth of the appointment. It must not be seen as a sinecure or as a last resting place before retirement.

Retaining a government affairs consultant (the author's occupation)
The main advantages of a consultant are that they are steeped in the business of government and will almost invariably have a wider network of contacts than an in-house appointee, due to their wider field of operation for clients in various sectors. They can also provide advice and execution on lobbying as well as monitoring. Although arguably more expensive per man hour than an in-house appointment, for a person of equivalent seniority, due to the profit element, it is possible to engage their services on a project basis and come to more flexible remuneration arrangements than is normal with a member of staff. Obviously, unless they have worked with clients in your sector before, they will need to go through a learning process about your

business and its problems. Experienced consultants can, and should, be expected to climb that learning curve quickly.

Relying upon your trade association
This course offers the advantage of knowledge about your sector, if not the detail of your company's problems, plus the significant fact that Whitehall will certainly target the trade associations in a sector for consultation on any matter affecting them. The main downside factor is that the competence of trade associations varies considerably and this is reflected in the real, as distinct from the formal, attention paid to their representations by Whitehall. In addition, the classic difficulty faced by trade associations is conflict of interest among their membership, which can lead to a lowest common denominator approach in their lobbying and this may be reflected in their monitoring. This can be highly unsatisfactory if the interests of your organization lie outside the common position.

Whichever approach is adopted, and many companies will use some combination of them, effective monitoring arises from:

- Clear definition of priority subjects
- Immediate attention to policy documents, discussion papers, seminars and the like, which set the terms of the debate in the earliest stages
- Feeding this intelligence in to the right levels of your organization; this may not, indeed usually should not, mean the chairman's office alone, but also the appropriate specialists within the company who are in a position to evaluate the precise potential implications
- Ensuring the opportunity for discussion of external developments. Mere circulation of paper without the evolution of a company viewpoint and response often degerates into an ill-regarded bureaucratic exercise
- Prompt registration of the company's interest in the subject to the departments, researchers, pressure groups etc., so as to ensure the opportunity for participation in the evolving debate

These requirements can be met by any or all of the methods mentioned, but the point is that, one way or another, they have to be met or else all the effort can be dissipated. The reality is that monitoring of government affairs has to be part of an active programme of representation if it is not to revert into a low cost gesture. Sadly, too many companies seem to be prepared to settle for the gesture.

PREPARATION

Probably more business representations fail to make an impact in Whitehall for lack of preparation than for any other reason. This arises not only from an insufficient appreciation on the part of business of the quite different perspectives of Ministers and thus officials (see below); but also from a predisposition by business to believe that their case is self-evident. All organizations to a greater or lesser degree fall into the trap of narcissism. Most businesses will communicate with Whitehall when they believe their interests are being affected adversely. Therefore their tone of voice is often complaining, and those charged with communicating will often be under internal pressure to produce results. These circumstances often produce peremptory and even rude demands for Government to cease and desist from the policy or behaviour or policy line complained of. This simply will not cut any ice in Whitehall, and can indeed be counterproductive. Communications with Whitehall should always be reasoned submissions. Facts and figures should be prepared and verified on the assumption that the recipient is a stranger to the sector. Bear in mind that the official dealing with the issue may only recently have arrived from another part of the Department and may have no background other than that gleaned from the file. A helpful note from you, setting out the facts, providing research results, and giving evidence, rather than assertions, for policy recommendations will be welcomed, and will establish your credentials as an interest to be acknowledged. Protest will be noted, but will not produce dialogue; bluster will be ignored.

RESEARCH

Although, in totality, Whitehall has considerable resources of knowledge, experience, facts and figures, the chances are that in your particular sector, on the matter which concerns you at a particular time, Whitehall's knowledge is incomplete. You should use this knowledge gap to your advantage, not just by providing a reasoned submission based on your own experience and interests, but also where possible, by buttressing that by independent evidence. A study by a reputable academic, management consultancy or opinion research organization, though commissioned by you, will carry weight. To be more effective, this research should not be, or appear to be, simply a rehearsal of your arguments against the 'widgets tax' under a different letterhead, but an examination, say, of the employment effects of the removal of the widgets tax, or a public opinion survey of consumers' attitudes to this tax compared with others, or a paper on alternative tax regimes in the sector, etc. With skill and discretion, such research findings can be brought into the public domain through the press and bring additional pressure to bear on Government to recognize your case. (See Chapter 28, Campaigning.)

APPROACH AT THE RIGHT LEVEL

Assuming you have identified the particular decision-making process which concerns you at an early stage, through your monitoring system, and equipped with rational argument, evidence and possibly independent research, where do you go first in Whitehall?

The answer will almost invariably be at the level where the work on particular issues is actually done, and as we have seen, this is at the grade 5 and grade 7 levels. It will be those officials – and only them – who will read every word of your submission and those of your trade association, competitors, the pressure groups, etc. It is at those levels that all this material is processed, advantages and disadvantages identified and the matter brought to a suitable state for Ministerial decision. Officials at a higher level in the chain of command will be informed and involved, but to a lesser degree. Their main function is not to be the experts on particular sectors, but to manage those who are; or to give close political support to Ministers; or to conduct major negotiations with other Whitehall departments or the EC, etc.

Although this division of labour is perfectly analogous to what happens in BP or ICI, it is sometimes made less obvious than it is by the public 'fronting' roles performed by more senior officials and by Ministers. As a matter of courtesy, officials at grade 3 level or above will, for example, lead the evidence given to a parliamentary select committee, or will host a meeting with senior representatives of a trade association. A Minister might even make the opening remarks at such a meeting, but will seldom if ever stay. This does not alter the location of the engine room. It must be noted that some businesspeople find these facts somewhat unpalatable and appear to cling to the old adage 'if you want something done, go to the man at the top'. It is true that if the chairman of a significant company asks to see a senior civil servant, he will normally be seen. If the businessperson has cause for complaint because of poor performance of an official at working level, (civil servants are human, can get over-promoted, have nervous breakdowns, etc., like the rest of us) then senior officials will become involved. Where the subject is massive (say the privatization of a major industry) and highly political, then probably a grade 2 official will be heavily involved, and be more evident at meetings, in correspondence, etc., but this is obviously exceptional. If and when an issue ripens, becomes more complex or more political, then more senior officials will become involved, and you will have dealings with them. None of this alters the fact that the best place to go first is the engine room of Whitehall, because, by and large, most issues of concern to businesses are, in the context of Whitehall, micro-issues.

HOW TO APPROACH AN OFFICIAL

Officials work harder than most businessmen think (and harder than many businesspeople, particularly during the passage of legislation). Do not waste their time. If starting from scratch, obtain a copy of the *Civil Service Year Book* (published annually by HMSO and stocked by most public libraries). This contains the names of all Ministers and officials down to grade 5, and in several cases, to grade 6 or 7, together with official addresses and contact telephone numbers. Beware, the *Year Book* is out of date as soon as it is printed. If your query is about the administration of an existing scheme or piece of legislation, say, your eligibility for a DTI grant; or about a local road-building project by DTP, or whether the DOE should be taking action against a polluter in your area; you should approach the regional offices of those departments, or the appropriate executive agency.

This sort of contact should be relatively straightforward. The legislation is in place, rules have been established and experience gained to a greater or lesser degree. Your task is not to lobby, but to enquire. It is worth noting that the regional directors of the departments mentioned above are not only the managers of their staff; they are also supposed to be the eyes and ears of their Ministers in their regions. They are therefore interested, particularly in the case of the DTI, in getting to know the problems and prospects of businesses in their part of the country. If you have a general point to make – of some substance – do not hesitate to write to the regional director for your area. Their offices can also assist you in contacting relevant Whitehall officials.

Let us suppose, however, that the matter concerning you is new policy rather than existing administration, and you want to contact the central Whitehall department yourself. Telephone to confirm the name of the grade 5 in the most likely sounding division of the relevant department, and establish that he is handling the issue of interest. Do not invite him to lunch. Write a brief letter to him setting out your concern and request a meeting.

If, due to pressure of work, you are offered a meeting with a grade 7 official, accept. The letter is preferable to a phone call pure and simple, especially if your company is not a household name, since it puts on the file your letterhead, your correct job title and the fact of your concern.

Take no more than an hour at the first meeting. Go prepared. Make your points and leave an aide-memoire setting out the relevant arguments, facts and figures. Establish from the official what the Government's objectives are, where the matter stands, whether or not legislation is planned, what the relevant timings are and which Minister is taking the lead. Find out if any consultation process is under way and ask to be included in it. Enquire whether there are any departmental advisory committees, with external members, relevant to the subject. Get the names of the members so that you can approach them. Do not hesitate to ask the official, if it is not clear to you, what political aspects are involved so that you have an understanding of the forces at work but, equally, do not parade your own political opinions: he will be unable to have a debate with you, and no useful purpose will be served. The meeting will be minuted and go on the file.

Depending on the complexity of the issue, this initial exchange should give you a good sense of what considerations are driving the Government, how well or badly your interests may be affected, where representations are coming from and how long you have to get your message across. Arrange to keep in touch with the official as the matter unfolds. Offer to provide information, technical advice, and site visits, if appropriate. Use him to establish the names of others involved in the process, whether in other Whitehall departments, the European Commission or the pressure groups. Such information will be made freely available to you and could save you a good deal of time.

How the relationship develops from that point depends very much on circumstances. Civil servants are not stamped out on a production line. Some will be more forthcoming than others. An official nursing a Bill through Parliament will be under immense time and other pressures, and may for that reason seem unhelpful. Some businesspeople feel uneasy if they have not achieved at an early stage some sort of social relationship with an important contact. Time permitting, civil servants will respond to lunch and dinner invitations, and even corporate entertainment at some cultural event. But this sort of contact, especially the latter, should be used with tact and discretion, and should never put an official in the slightest perceived danger of being compromised. Do not give gifts (other than the tawdry plastic paperweights your chairman has spent so much time designing).

Social contact should be the courteous extension of an established businesslike relationship, not the start of it.

DEALING WITH MINISTERS

From your monitoring and your established contact with officials you should know whether or not things are going your way. If they are, there is no need to feel, as a matter of form, that you need to make representations to Ministers. As we have seen, their diaries are overloaded and they will not thank you for a pointless waste of their time. Ministers are decision makers, but above all they are politicians. You need to approach them when the signs are that they could be disposed to take a decision which would be against your interests. This may arise from their being inadequately briefed on the effect on business of the 'wrong' decision. Equally, they may be perfectly well briefed on that but are politically inclined to do a deal with their counterparts in the EC, or to accede to the representations of environmentalists, consumer organizations or, not to mince matters, they may be making a decision based on a judgment of the effect on their own political standing in their party.

This is not meant to be a cynical or censorious commentary. The business of politicians is politics; and the stuff of politics is winning votes, faulting your opponents, doing deals, gaining and keeping power. These are facts; and the businessman should constantly bear them in mind when dealing with politicians. On many business subjects, on many occasions, the political reading will be low or transient; sometimes it will be high and long lasting; but it will always be there.

Politicians have a different basic perspective from businesspeople. You do not need to share it in order to take commonsense precautions in your dealing with Ministers. Show that you have a realistic understanding of the need to show concern for the interests of the consumers, or the environment, or whatever factor appears to be dominant in the Minister's mind, even if the arguments presented are incorrect. Point out errors, of course, but seek to provide some ammunition from your specialist knowledge with which the Minister may defend himself if he adopts your position – e.g., generating employment, winning export orders, remaining competitive, encouraging new technology, etc.

Recognize that you may not win. If the matter is important enough, you may have to mount a campaign which puts overt pressure on the Minister (see Chapter 28). Let us suppose, however, that matters have not reached that stage. You may be unsure whether your case has been fully and correctly communicated to the Minister, or it may look as if he is inclining to yield to pressure from another quarter. You need to meet him to satisfy yourself that your case is made authoritatively and receives a fair hearing. How do you do it?

Do it formally. Do not attempt to buttonhole a Minister socially or at a party conference, etc. A Minister, as decision maker, can only function within the structure of his advisers (which include political advisers). Therefore ask the official with whom you have been dealing to arrange the meeting. They will do this through the Minister's Private Office. All Ministers have such an office, headed by a Private Secretary who is a young high-flier. He organizes the Minister's day and the flow of paperwork to and from him. If for some reason you need to see the Minister, write directly to the Private Secretary. He will pass the correspondence to the officials dealing with the matter, who may or may not recommend that he sees you. If you are not offered a meeting, you should seek help from your constituency MP, or an MP who specialises in the subject concerned, to· arrange a meeting, which that MP would expect to attend and front.

However you get to see the Minister, be brief. Assume you will have no more than half an hour. Make it crystal clear what you would like the Minister to do or not to do. Leave time for questions and discussion. Do not use visual aids. Leave an *aide-memoire* setting out your case, plus relevant facts and figures; but if this has previously been done with officials, a one page note setting out the basic points will suffice. It also should contain a clear statement of the desired outcome. The Minister will be accompanied by his Private Secretary, who will not speak, and one or more officials from the division dealing with the matter, who may. The latter will have submitted a brief before the meeting, will discuss it after your departure with the Minister and will be responsible for any follow-up. If you have not previously met them, contact them afterwards to make a belated attempt to establish a dialogue. Write a courtesy letter to the Minister subsequently, but if there has been any substantial comment, undertaking or agreement on his part, make sure to record it in the letter in clear and accurate terms with embellishment.

28
Campaigning

This chapter deals with the methods required to deal with the most difficult situations presented to business by Whitehall. These are, for example, government positions, the abandonment of which would cost the exchequer significant amounts of revenue; manifesto commitments of particular significance to important sections of the party; positions which have emerged out of tortuous internal and/or external political deals; government commitments given to consumer or environmental interests with considerable political clout, etc.

Situations like these need special attention. Normal representations as outlined in the previous chapter will not be enough to change entrenched attitudes; a campaign will be necessary. There is no generally accepted definition of this term. It is used here broadly to denote a set of activities which:

- Are designed to put pressure on decision makers over a period of time
- Are overt, at least in part
- Are planned and managed professionally
- Use a variety of communications techniques
- Involve a number of participants orchestrated by the prime mover

It is not unusual for the prime mover to be one organization, large enough to afford the resources necessary for such an operation and sufficiently skilled to manage it. The major consumer and environmental pressure groups certainly fall into this category and some, indeed, refer explicitly to their 'campaigning' work. However, many of their objectives are of a different order to those of business. Typically, they seek to get the Government to take new action, e.g., new safety standards for certain products, whereas many business campaigns seek the repeal of damaging legislation. Some large companies can and do mount campaigns over what they regard as vital issues. More common are groups of organizations, trade associations or consortia. Any company can use the principles of campaigning, discussed below, to advance its cause.

A REALISTIC TIMETABLE

A campaign will not succeed unless its promoters accept from the start that a government with a healthy majority will not wish to be seen to reverse its position overnight, particularly in response to a visible special interest lobby. Time will be needed to allow the Government to change its position in an apparently considered fashion. Changes requiring legislation will have to wait until time can be found in the parliamentary calendar. Changes to Finance Act legislation will normally have to conform at least to the annual Budget cycle, and more realistically will take a minimum of two years. Therefore do not embark upon a campaign unless you and any co-campaigners are aware of its likely duration, and are prepared to stick it out. Persistence in campaigning is a virtue which needs to be prominently displayed to government. If you stop campaigning before you have achieved your objective, or some acceptable settlement, you will be regarded as having withdrawn your case.

RECRUIT ALLIES

A company with a grievance is more likely to obtain a hearing if it is joined by others similarly affected. Two trade associations are better than one, and so on. (When dealing with the European Commission, it is vital to demonstrate that the problem is not just for UK companies but is Community-wide, or at least affects several member states.) Broadening the support also increases the resources available, human and financial.

BUILD COALITIONS

It is important, as far as possible, to avoid the appearance of a narrow vested interest. The Government will feel more comfortable in acceding to the request of a group enjoying wider public support. For example, bus operators have successfully involved Womens' Institutes in a campaign concerning rural bus routes. The nuclear industry has strong support from the craft unions (who are, of course, visibly representative of workers in many other industries). The motor manufacturing industry has obtained the endorsement of the road hauliers, freight transport operators and motorists' organizations in its campaigning activities.

Remember that, in business campaigning, you are almost always seeking to convey a message Government does not wish to hear and you are always competing for their attention with other, more popular, campaigns. Make it difficult for politicians to say 'It's only the widgets manufacturers moaning again'. Coalitions provide a defence against that gambit.

CREATE BACK-BENCH POLITICAL AWARENESS

It must be the aim of all campaigns to seek to exert pressure on government via their own back-bench supporters. (There is little point generally in concentrating on opposition members, since they can hardly carry weight with the administration they seek to replace.) As discussed previously in Part 3: Lobbying Parliament, back-benchers are subject to continuous lobbying from interests of every kind. In general, business issues are the least politically interesting of all the representations they hear – apart from obvious exceptions like a factory closure in a Member's constituency.

Traditional parliamentary lobbyists tend to express their purpose as to 'organize back-bench support' for their client's case. The business lobbyist has to try much harder than the lobbyist from, say, a charity (of which there are many) since it is clearly much more obviously in the political self-interest of an MP to declare himself 'in support' of tax relief for charities than for industrialists. In this, as in other aspects of campaigning, the terminology employed is important. In the United States, where lobbying is highly developed, there is, for example, an organization called the Council for Energy Awareness. It is in fact a nuclear industry lobby: but clearly it is easier for a congressman to receive, listen to and possibly support an organization thus named than 'the Nuclear Industry Association'.

Therefore in dealing with Government back-bench MPs, care must be taken to present the campaign identity and objectives in a politically appropriate language. Simply making a presentation about the iniquities of the widgets tax and asking for their support for its repeal is unlikely to be productive. Bear in mind that you are asking them, in effect, to challenge the policies of the Government they are pledged to support, a fact that they can be forcefully reminded of by their whips if they cause too much trouble. It is more realistic to aim to get them to express 'concern' about the problem you have identified rather than support for your campaign. (Again, the language used can help produce this effect. The CBI campaigned long and hard – and unsuccessfully – against the National Insurance Surcharge, until they started calling it the 'Jobs Tax'. MPs and the media then started to take notice and put pressure on the Government to remove it, which they did.)

The main ways in which a campaign can involve numbers of back-bench MPs in the task of transmitting a message to government are:

Linkman schemes

At constituency level: one of the most effective methods, employed by the CBI, the Society of Motor Manufacturers and Traders and other leading industry bodies is a 'Linkman Scheme'. This involves the creation of a network of representatives of member companies of the industry body, organized according to parliamentary constituencies and charged with forming a link with their local MPs. The industry body, centrally, agrees that the main plank in its campaigning platform over a period is, say, the abolition of a certain tax. The body's economists work up an analysis of the defects of the tax, with special attention given to politically interesting aspects, such as employment implications. The network of 'linkmen' is recruited and briefed. They are deputed to write to their local MPs in their own words, requesting a meeting. At the meeting they advance the same broad arguments about the tax, but they lend verisimilitude in a way which the same brief sent to the MP from the headquarters of the body cannot do. The MP can, for example, visualize the local company Linkman taking on a few more employees in a much more vivid way than through reading the formal economic analysis of the employment aspects of the tax.

Finally, the Linkman is asked to request the MP to write, in his own words, to the relevant Minister. Some poorly managed campaigns provide standard letters. These are instantly recognized as such by Government and ignored. The secret is to get the basic idea across to the MP and leave it to him to express it naturally, with his own nuances. A Minister will feel obliged to respond to a letter from any MP, and in a considered fashion to one of his own colleagues. Officials draft the replies, and here the strength of a non-standard letter shows. The official is forced to think afresh about the merits of the tax, and the strengths of the traditional departmental or Treasury arguments for retaining it if he is replying to separate, individual formulations of the problem. Naturally he will be aware that it is no coincidence that a large number of letters starts to arrive on the subject but he will nonetheless not be able to ignore them. Attention and awareness will have been raised, which is the object of the exercise. Plainly, this sort of operation requires a fair degree of management, but can be very effective.

Back-bench party committees

As discussed in Part III, each parliamentary party has informal groupings of back-benchers interested in particular subjects, e.g., trade and industry, agriculture, etc., and there are also a number of all-party back-bench groups, e.g., the Parliamentary and Scientific Committee, or the all-party Roads Group. No campaign operating in their area of interest can afford to ignore these groups. They exist in order to be informed and therefore it is a straightforward matter to approach their office-bearers and offer a presentation. They have no fixed membership; meetings are attended by those MPs who wish to learn about the particular subject. Be prepared for a poor attendance on the day. Consult one of the office bearers in advance about likely interest and keep in touch with him about the arrangements for the presentation, if one is arranged. A typical format would be a one-hour presentation at 11.30 a.m., followed by a buffet lunch, both in a room at the House of Commons or nearby. Also be prepared for nothing concrete to emerge from such a meeting. It is possible to seek to use the presentation to stimulate the tabling of a Question or Motion, as discussed in Chapter 20, but before contemplating this, specialist advice from a Parliamentary consultant should be sought.

Departmental select committees

Departmental select committees are part of the formal machinery of Parliament and as such must be approached by campaigners with care and respect. They must not be asked to put down Questions, write letters, or anything of that kind. The advantage of interesting a select committee in your campaign is that select committee reports are always replied to by the Government, though not necessarily heeded; and may be the subject of a short debate.

Representations from a campaign will sit most comfortably with a select committee if it is already examining a relevant area. For example, representations by the motor industry to the Select Committee on Trade and Industry about the Special Car Tax, when the committee was investigating the automotive components sector, produced a recommendation in the Committee's report for the abolition of the tax. Again, if the matter is of high public interest, a select committee will be disposed to hear evidence. For example, the Select Committee on Transport agreed to receive presentations from the various contenders offering different solutions to the Channel Fixed Link project. The best approach is through the clerk to the appropriate select committee – a House of Commons official whose name can be obtained from the Public Information Office. You should offer 'to provide evidence' on the subject concerned. Depending on the closeness of fit with the work programme of the committee, and on timing (there can occasionally be short hiatuses in their work), you may be invited to provide a written note; appear before the committee formally; or the committee may accept an invitation to visit a site, or hear a presentation outside the House.

USE THE MEDIA

Campaigning invariably involves the skills of public relations as well as government relations. This is a natural and inevitable outcome and should not cause regrets or misgivings, provided a high standard of professionalism is maintained throughout. The two subjects are in reality simply different expressions of the art of communications. The historic public relations skill of media relations is central. There can be no campaign if there is no media coverage. Indeed politicians – who are avid followers of the media – will largely define the existence and strength of a campaign with reference to whether and how it is reported.

Journalists require factual material, access to the personalities involved in the campaign and prompt information about new developments. Broadcast journalists require, in addition, sound and pictures. All of them are employed to write or broadcast stories; therefore avoid off the record briefings wherever possible. The sort of campaign mounted by business will typically be covered by a business or industrial correspondent rather than a general news reporter. Depending on the subject, it might, alternatively, be covered by a specialist writer on, say, transport.

You need to make it both easy and professionally satisfying for the journalists to stay with your campaign. Therefore long–term relations have to be built up, regular and effective contacts maintained, reliable information supplied, and new slants introduced. The basic messages will probably remain unchanged throughout the campaign, therefore, the newsworthiness has to be maintained by new examples of your theme, fresh members of the campaign appearing with a story to tell, independent researchers' work presented, new visits organized, etc.

CREATE COMMUNICATIONS TOOLS

Your target audiences in government, the media, your campaign supporters, all need to be assisted and prompted to keep the campaign messages in mind. The ideas therefore have to receive concrete expression in a variety of ways, including:

- Booklets
- Briefing papers on particular aspects
- Videos
- Educational material for schools
- Selective mailing lists for the distribution of the above
- A speakers' bureau of campaign members to accept speaking invitations
- Exhibition material for use both at appropriate industry exhibitions and as background 'dressing' for speeches, meetings, press briefings, etc.

Appendix A
Further Reading
and Reference

GENERAL

Hennessy, P. (1989) *Whitehall*, London: Secker & Warbung

Hennessy, P. (1986) *Cabinet*, Oxford: Blackwell

Drewer and Butcher (1988) *The Civil Service Today*, Oxford: Blackwell

Kellner & Crowther-Hunt (1980) The Civil Servants: An Enquiry into Britain's Ruling Class, London: Macdonald

Young & Sloman (1982) *No Minister: An Enquiry into the Civil Service*, London: BBC

Young & Sloman (1984) *But Chancellor: An Enquiry into the Treasury*, London: BBC

Jenkins & Sloman (1985) *With Respect, Ambassador: An Enquiry into the Foreign Office*, London: BBC

Blackstone, T. and Plowden, W., (1988) *Inside the Think Tank: Advising the Cabinet 1971–1983*, London: Heinemann

Top Jobs in Whitehall: Appointments and Promotions in the Civil Service. Report of a RIPA Working Group 1987

The Civil Service Year Book, London: HMSO annually

Public Administration. Published quarterly for the Royal Institute of Public Administration by Blackwell

Miller, C., (1987) *Lobbying Government: Understanding and Influencing the Corridors of Power*, Oxford: Blackwell

Departmental Reports: Each government department publishes a report presenting its expenditure plans for the future and reporting performance against previous plans. HMSO annually

Rose, Professor R, (1991) *Too much Reshuffling of the Cabinet Pack?*, London,

Institute of Economic Affairs
British Overseas Aid: Opportunities for Business. ODA 1991
Englefield, D., (1985) *Parliament – Whitehall and Westminster, Government Informs Parliament: The Changing Scene.* London: Longman

CHAPTER 2: EUROPEAN COMMUNITY

Directory of the European Communities. Published annually by the Office for Official Publications of the European Communities. Available in UK from HMSO.
Colchester & Buchan (1990) *Europe Relaunched: Truths and Illusions on the way to 1992,* London: The Economist Books and Century Business

The DTI has an extensive range of publications to help British business prepare for the single market environment in the EC. A *Single Market Information Pack* is regularly updated, and is available from all DTI Regional Offices (see Appendix D). In addition, an on-line data-base on single market information, entitled Spearhead, is available. This summarizes all current and prospective EC measures in the single market programme and in other areas which will have substantial implications for business, including collaborative EC R&D programmes; and EC measures on health and safety at work, the environment and the social dimension of the single market. It provides details of measures which have been adopted, proposals currently under discussion in Brussels, and other proposals which the Commission intend to submit.

Spearhead gives the name and telephone number of the official in Whitehall responsible for each measure. It can also be used to access the full text of relevant adopted legislation. The information on the data-base is updated weekly. Many chambers of commerce, trade associations and libraries subscribe to services which have access to Spearhead.

Information on the EC can be obtained from
– The European Commission (London Office) 071-973 1992
– The European Parliament (London Office) 071-222 0411
– UKREP (Brussels) 010 322 230 6205

CHAPTER 5: DTI

DTI: A Guide for Business. This lists contacts in Regional Offices and in the Central Policy Divisions, with names and telephone numbers, and is regularly updated. Available from DTI centrally and locally. For copies write to DTI (Dept 2D), FREEPOST LONDON SW1V 1YX or telephone your Regional Office (See Appendix D)

- Publications
  A listing of DTI publications published by the Department is available as above. Most DTI and other government departments are published by HMSO. Daily, monthly and annual listings of HMSO publications are available from HMSO bookshops or from: HMSO Publications Centre, PO Box 276, LONDON SW8 5DT.
- Non-HMSO DTI publications are listed monthly in *Business Briefing*, a weekly publication of the Association of British Chambers of Commerce; (subscription enquiries to Border House, High Street, Farndon, Chester CH3 9PK).

CHAPTER 6 DEPARTMENT OF EMPLOYMENT

1990s The Skills Decade. Department of Employment 1990.

CHAPTER 7 DEPARTMENT OF ENVIRONMENT

General
Lowe & Woyder (1983) *Environmental Groups in Politics*, London: Allen & McCormick (1991) *British Politics and the Environment*, Earthscan
Environmental Contacts, a Guide for Business. DTI 1991
MINIS: Departmental management information document; copies held at DoE Library, 2 Marsham Street, London.

Environmental Protection
Environmental Protection Act 1990. HMSO
This Common Inheritance. Britain's Environmental Strategy (Environment White Paper Cm 1200) HMSO 1990

Inner Cities
Renewing the Cities: A Report on the DoE Inner City Programme 1989–90. Dept of Environment 1990

Construction
Euronews Construction published quarterly by *Building* magazine on behalf of the DoE.

CHAPTER 8 DEPARTMENT OF TRANSPORT

Transport – a guide to the Department. (Available free from the Public Enquiry Unit, Room P1/035, Department of Transport, 2 Marsham Street, London SW1P 2EB)
Departmental Mangement Plan 1990–91. April 1990. (Available from MSSD, Department of Transport, Room 1141, Millbank Tower, 21–24 Millbank, London SW1 4QU)
Department of Transport Report CM 1507 HMSO (This report contains a more detailed bibliography)

CHAPTER 9 HM TREASURY

Barnett, J. (1982) *Inside the Treasury*, London: Deutsch
Heclo & Wildavsky, (1981) *The Private Government of Public Money*, London: Macmillan
Thain C. & Wright M. *Planning and Controlling Public Expenditure in the UK, Part I: The Treasury's Public Expenditure Survey.* In Public Administration 70, 3–24.
Pliatsky, L., (1984) *Getting and Spending: Public Expenditure, Employment and Inflation*, Oxford: Blackwell.

Competition Bodies
An Outline of United Kingdom Competition Policy. OFT. 1990.
Annual Report of the Director General of Fair Trading. HMSO annually (contains details of all publications during the year).
Monopolies and Mergers Commission: the Role of the Commission. 3rd edition, HMSO 1990. (also contains a reading list).
Monopolies and Mergers Commission Annual Review. HMSO annually.
OFTEL, OFWAT, OFFER, OFGAS Annual Reports, HMSO

CHAPTER 17 NEDO

The National Economic Office. NEDO. 1991.

CHAPTERS 18–22 LOBBYING PARLIAMENT

The Public Information Office of the House of Commons (071-219 4272) answers questions from the public on all aspects of parliamentary business, and publishes Factsheets on a wide range of parliamentary subjects.

The House of Lords Information Office (071-219 3107) provides a similar service for the House of Lords.

Dods Parliamentary Companion Annually. 60 Chandos Place, London, WC2N 4HG.

Vacher's Parliamentary Companion Quarterly.

Smith, M. (1982) *Lobbying: An Introduction to Political Communication in the UK.* Countrywide Political Communications; 29 Tufton Street, London SW1P 3QL.

Patterson, B. (1991) *Lobbying: An Introduction to Political Communications in Europe.* Countrywide Political Communications; 29 Tufton Street, London SW1P 3QL.

CHAPTER 26: ECO-LABELLING

House of Commons Environment Committee. Eighth Report: Eco-labelling. Vols I & II. HMSO. HC 474 I-II 1991.

CHAPTER 28 CAMPAIGNING

The Campaign Guide. Public Policy Unit, 50 Rochester Row, London SW1P 113. 1991.

Appendix B
European Commission:
Directorates General

DIRECTORATE-GENERAL I

External Relations

Directorate A GATT, OECD, commercial questions with respect to agriculture, fisheries, export credit policy and export promotion, internal market.

Directorate B Relations with North America, Australia, South Africa and New Zealand.

Directorate C General questions and instruments of external economic policy.

Directorate D Sectoral commercial questions, computerized economic analysis, and external relations in the research, science and nuclear energy fields.

Directorate E Relations with Central Europe and Oriental countries, USSR and CSCE, multilateral questions; 6–24 co-ordination. Aid programme to Central and Eastern Europe.

Directorate F Relations with China, Japan, and other countries of the Far East.

Directorate G Relations with EFTA and bilateral relations with States of North and Central Europe other than State trading countries.

Directorate H Mediterranean, Near and Middle East.

Directorate I Latin America.

Directorate J Asia (except China, South Korea, Japan, Macao and Hong Kong).

Directorate K North–South relations.

External Delegations External delegations to international organizations. External delegations to third countries.

DIRECTORATE-GENERAL II

Economic and Financial Affairs
Directorate A National Economies.
Directorate B Economic evaluation of Community policies.
Directorate C Macro-economic analyses and policies.
Directorate D Monetary matters.
Directorate E Financial engineering and capital movements.

DIRECTORATE-GENERAL III

Internal market and industrial affairs
Directorate A General Affairs.
Directorate B Horizontal Instruments of internal market.
Directorate C Internal market and industrial affairs I.
Directorate D Internal market and industrial affairs II.
Directorate E Internal market and industrial affairs III.
Directorate F Approximation of laws, freedom of establishment and freedom to provide services; the professions.

DIRECTORATE-GENERAL IV

Competition
Directorate A General competition policy and co-ordination.
Directorate B Restrictive practices, abuse of dominant positions and other distortions of competition I.
Directorate C Restrictive practices, abuse of dominant positions and other distortions of competition II.
Directorate D Restrictive practices, abuse of dominant positions and other distortions of competition III.
Directorate E State aids. Merger Task Force.

DIRECTORATE-GENERAL V

Employment, Industrial Relations and Social Affairs
Directorate A Industrial relations and social dialogue.
Directorate B Employment and labour market.
Directorate C Social security, social protection and living conditions.
Directorate D European Social Fund
Directorate E Health and safety.

Task Force for Human Resources, Education, Training and Youth.

DIRECTORATE-GENERAL VI

Agriculture
Directorate A General matters, relations with the European Parliament and the Economic and Social Committee.
Directorate B I Agro-Economical Legislation.
Directorate B II Quality and health.
Directorate C Organization of markets in crop products.
Directorate D Organization of markets in livestock products.
Directorate E Organization of markets in specialized crops.
Directorate F I Rural development I.
Directorate F II Rural development II.
Directorate G European Agricultural Guidance and Guarantee Fund.
Directorate H International affairs relating to agriculture.

DIRECTORATE-GENERAL VII

Transport
Directorate A Maritime transport; transport economics; legislation.
Directorate B Inland transport; market analysis; transport safety; research and technology.
Directorate C Air transport, transport infrastructure, social and ecological aspects of transport.

DIRECTORATE-GENERAL VIII

Development
Directorate A Development activities and trade policy.
Directorate B West and Central Africa; Caribbean.
Directorate C East and Southern Africa; the Indian Ocean; Pacific.
Directorate D Management of instruments.
Directorate E Finance.

Task Force for the Negotiations (TFN) of the next Convention.

DIRECTORATE-GENERAL IX

Personnel and Administration

Directorate **RO** Personnel I.
Directorate **C** Personnel II – careers.
Directorate **GA** General administration.
Directorate **I** Informatics.
Directorate **DAD** Administration of delegations and information offices.

TRANSLATION SERVICE

Directorate General and Language matters.
Translation – Brussels
A. General and administrative affairs, budget and financial control.
B. Economic and financial affairs, internal market and industrial affairs.
C. Agricultural, fisheries, regional policy and structural policies.
D. External relations, transport, customs union and development.
E. Technology, energy, environment and consumer.

Translation – Luxembourg
F. Social affairs and tenders.
G. Statistical Office, general affairs (Luxembourg) and inter-institutional questions.

DIRECTORATE-GENERAL X

Audio-visual, Information, Communication and Culture
Directorate **A** Audiovisual.
Directorate **B** Information.
Directorate **C** Culture communications and people's Europe.

DIRECTORATE-GENERAL XI

Environment, Consumer Protection and Nuclear Safety
Directorate **A** Nuclear safety, industry and the environment, civil protection.
Directorate **B** Environment Quality and Natural Resources.
Directorate **C** Environmental Instruments and International Affairs.

DIRECTORATE-GENERAL XII

Science, Research and Development
Directorate **A** Scientific and technological policy.

Directorate B Means of action.
Directorate C Technological research.
Directorate D Nuclear safety research.
Directorate E Environment and non-nuclear energy.
Directorate F Biology.
Directorate G Scientific and technical co-operation with non-member countries.
Directorate H Support of S/T-policy Fusion programme.

Joint Research Centre

DIRECTORATE-GENERAL XIII

Telecommunications, Information Industries and Innovation
Directorate A Information technology – Esprit.
Directorate B Information industry and market.
Directorate C Exploitation of research and technological development, technology transfer and innovation.
Directorate D Telecommunication policy.
Directorate E General affairs.
Directorate F RACE programme and development of advanced telematics services.

DIRECTORATE-GENERAL XIV

Fisheries
Directorate A Budget general affairs.
Directorate B Markets and external resources.
Directorate C Internal resources and monitoring.
Directorate D Structures.

DIRECTORATE-GENERAL XV

Financial institutions and company law
Directorate A Financial institutions.
Directorate B Company law, company and capital movements taxation.

DIRECTORATE-GENERAL XVI

Regional policies
Directorate A Guidelines and priorities.

Directorate B Development (Object 1).
Directorate C Development (Object 1).
Directorate D Industrial zones in decline, rural zones reconversion ECSC (Object 2).
Directorate E Financial management.

DIRECTORATE-GENERAL XVII

Energy
Directorate A Energy policy.
Directorate B Industries and markets I: fossil fuels.
Directorate C Industries and markets II: non-fossil energy.
Directorate D Energy technology.
Directorate E Euratom Safeguards.

DIRECTORATE-GENERAL XVIII

Credit and Investments
Directorate A Finance and accounting.
Directorate B Investment and loans.

DIRECTORATE-GENERAL XIX

Budgets
Directorate A Expenditure.
Directorate B Resources.
Directorate C Budget execution.

DIRECTORATE-GENERAL XX

Financial control
Directorate A Questions of principle: control of operating, research and co-operation expenditure.
Directorate B FEDER, FSE, FEOGA and PIM – control of revenue, borrowing and lending operations, financial engineering and movement of funds.
Directorate C Control of receipts – FEOGA – guarantees and benefit assistance.

Directorate-General XXI

Customs union and indirect taxation
Directorate A External tariff questions.
Directorate B Customs union legislation.
Directorate C Indirect taxation including elimination of fiscal frontiers.

Directorate-General XXII

Co-ordination of structural policies
Directorate Co-ordination, monitoring and evaluation of structural policies.

Directorate-General XXIII

Enterprise policy, commerce, tourism and social economy

Appendix C
Executive Agencies
Established and Planned

EXECUTIVE AGENCIES ESTABLISHED (OCTOBER 1991)

	Employees
Accounts Services Agency	90
Building Research Establishment	690
Cadw (Welsh Historic Monuments)	220
Central Office of Information	680
Central Veterinary Laboratory	600
Chemical and Biological Defence Establishment	600
Civil Service College	230
Companies House	1,100
Defence Research Agency	12,300
Directorate General of Defence Accounts	2,150
Driver and Vehicle Licensing Agency	5,250
Driving Standards Agency	2,100
Employment Service	34,500
Forensic Science Service	600
Historic Royal Palaces	340
Historic Scotland	610
HMSO	3,250
Hydrographic Office	870
Insolvency Service	1,500
Intervention Board	940
Laboratory of the Government Chemist	340
Land Registry	10,050
Medicines Control Agency	310

Meteorological Office	2,300
Military Survey	1,230
National Engineering Laboratory	380
National Physical Laboratory	830
National Weights and Measures Laboratory	50
Natural Resources Institute	420
NHS Estates	120
Occupational Health Service	100
Ordnance Survey	2,450
Patent Office	1,200
Queen Elizabeth II Conference Centre	70
Radiocommunications Agency	500
RAF Maintenance	13,000
Rate Collection Agency (Northern Ireland)	270
Recruitment and Assessment Services Agency	260
Registers of Scotland	1,200
Royal Mint	1,050
Scottish Fisheries Protection Agency	200
Service Children's Schools (North West Europe)	2,330
Social Security Agency (Northern Ireland)	5,500
Social Security Benefits Agency	65,600
Social Security Contributions Agency	7,200
Social Security Information Technology Services Agency	3,600
Social Security Resettlement Agency	470
The Buying Agency	80
Training & Employment Agency (Northern Ireland)	1,700
UK Passport Agency	1,200
Valuation Office	5,250
Vehicle Certification Agency	80
Vehicle Inspectorate	1,850
Veterinary Medicines Directorate	80
Warren Spring Laboratory	310
Wilton Park Conference Centre	30
	200,230

EXECUTIVE AGENCIES PLANNED – OCTOBER 1991

ADAS Agency	2,500
Agricultural Scientific Services	140

Central Science Laboratory	350
Central Statistical Office	1,050
Chessington Computer Centre	450
Child Support Agency (Northern Ireland)	not yet known
Common Services Division	1,730
Criminal Compensation (Northern Ireland)	140
Defence Animal Centre	140
Defence Operational Analysis Establishment	180
Defence Statistics Organization	170
Directorate Information Technology Bureau Services	120
Driver and Vehicle Testing Agency (N. Ireland)	250
Drivers Vehicles and Operators Information Technology	00
Duke of York's Royal Military School	100
Fire Service College	190
Fuel Suppliers' Branch	20
MOD Police	4,260
Naval Aircraft Repair Organization	1,470
Ordnance Survey (Northern Ireland)	200
Pesticide Safety Division	160
Planning Inspectorate	630
Property Holdings Portfolio Management	420
Public Record Office	440
Queen Victoria School	60
RAF Training	11,450
Royal Parks	580
Scottish Prisons	4,000
Social Security Child Support Agency	not yet known
Teachers' Pensions Branch	290
Transport Road Research Laboratory	580
Youth Treatment Service	210
	34,380

Appendix D
DTI Organization

DTI Regional Organization

DTI Headquarters
Ashdown House,
123 Victoria Street, London SW1E 6RB
Telephone 071-215 5000

DTI North East
Northumberland, Tyne and Wear, Durham and Cleveland.
Main Office, Stanegate House,
2 Groat Market, Newcastle upon Tyne NE1 1YN
Telephone 091-232 4722

DTI North West
Cheshire, Lancashire, Merseyside, Greater Manchester, Cumbria and the
High Peak District of Derbyshire

Manchester Office
All of the North West Region except for the area covered by the Liverpool
Office.
Sunley Tower, Piccadilly Plaza, Manchester M1 4BA
Telephone 061-236 2171

Liverpool Office
Travel to Work areas of Liverpool, Widnes/Runcorn, Wirral/Chester and
Wigan/St Helens.
Graeme House, Derby Square, Liverpool L2 7UP
Telephone 051-227 4111

DTI Yorkshire and Humberside
North Yorkshire
South Yorkshire
West Yorkshire and Humberside
Main Office
25 Queen Street, Leeds LS1 2TW
Telephone 0532 443171

DTI – East Midlands
Nottinghamshire, Derbyshire (except the High Peak), Leicestershire,
Lincolnshire, Northamptonshire.
Main Office
Severns House, 20 Middle Pavement, Nottingham NG1 7DW
Telephone 0602 506181

DTI – West Midlands
The Metropolitan Districts of Birmingham, Coventry, Dudley, Sandwell,
Solihull, Walsall and Wolverhampton and the Counties of Warwickshire,
Staffordshire, Shropshire and Hereford and Worcester.
Main Office
77 Paradise Circus, Queensway, Birmingham B1 2DT
Telephone 021-212 5000

DTI – South West
Cornwall (including Isles of Scilly), Devon, Somerset, Dorset, Wiltshire,
Gloucestershire and Avon.
Main Office
The Pithay, Bristol BS1 2PB

DTI – South East
Greater London, Berkshire, Buckinghamshire, Hampshire, Isle of Wight,
Kent, Oxfordshire, Surrey, East and West Sussex.
Main Office
Bridge Place, 88–89 Eccleston Square, London SW1V 1PT
Telephone 071-828 1105

DTI – East
Bedfordshire, Cambridgeshire, Essex, Herts, Norfolk, Suffolk.
Main Office
Building A, Westbrook Centre, Milton Road, Cambridge CB4 1YG
Telephone 0223 461941

The regional organization of the DTI only covers England. The equivalent organizations in Scotland, Wales and Northern Ireland are:

The Scottish Office Industry Department
New St Andrew's House, Edinburgh EH1 3TA
Telephone 031-556 8400

The Welsh Office Industry Department
Cathays Park, Cardiff CF1 3NQ
Telephone 0222 825111

Department of Economic Development Northern Ireland
Netherleigh, Massey Avenue, Belfast BT4 2JP
Telephone 0232 763244

Appendix E
The Industry and
Parliament Trust

The Industry and Parliament Trust (IPT) was founded in 1977 on the initiative of a group of industrialists concerned about the gap of understanding between industry and Parliament. In July 1977 every MP received a letter saying that the IPT had been formed, with two objectives:

- to enable Members of both Houses of Parliament and of the European Parliament to widen their experience in, and increase their knowledge of, industry
- to improve the understanding of industrial managers about the problems of Parliament in dealing with matters affecting industry.

The letter invited applications from Parliamentarians for Fellowships and immediately 49 applications – from all parties – were received. As of October 1991, 178 MPs, peers, MEPs and Officers of both Houses have completed the 25-day study programme in member companies of the Trust.

In addition, several other types of activity have been devised to enable managers employed by member companies to learn more about Parliament and government. For example company seminars have been organized, whereby company personnel are briefed on current parliamentary and political matters; and a parliamentary study programme for industrialists has been instituted where company nominees spend time with MPs and ministers and observe their work at first hand.

The IPT has extended its purview to Brussels, and maintains links with similar organizations abroad, many of which have based their practices on UK experience. The IPT is an educational charity, financed by the subscriptions of member companies (currently £4700 per annum), but companies do not elect Fellows; this is done by the independent trustees. The IPT meets any expenses incurred by Fellows. No payment is made by the companies to fellows.

Further information on the activities of the IPT may be obtained from its Secretariat at: 1 Buckingham Place, London SW1E 6HR. Tel: 071-976 5311.

Appendix F
The Whitehall and
Industry Group

The Whitehall & Industry Group places high calibre senior civil servants on short attachments to industry and commerce. The Group was founded in 1984 as a joint venture between industrialists and the Cabinet Office. It is a non-profit-making charity jointly funded by the government and the company members and has no political connections.

Objectives
The aims of the Group are to:

- give civil servants first-hand experience of industry and commerce and so encourage them to be more responsive to its needs
- offer valuable business experience to successful senior civil servants holding top posts to develop their management skills and understanding of corporate strategy
- increase amongst company members understanding of the functions and processes of government in both the UK and the EEC
- foster a dialogue between industry and commerce and government on non-political matters of mutual interest

Candidates
The candidates are generally high calibre civil servants between grade 5 (Assistant Secretary) and grade 3 (Under Secretary). Most are in their 30s and 40s. Typical industrial equivalents are Senior Manager for grade 5 and Director for grade 3.

All candidates have wide experience within their department, or even a number of departments, often including a spell in a Minister's private office. Candidates are also taken onto the scheme at a similar level from other public bodies such as the Bank of England.

Member Companies

Member companies are drawn from all areas of business within the UK. Company members are asked to arrange one attachment of three weeks' duration each year for a Civil Service candidate chosen in consultation with the Whitehall & Industry Group Directors. The programmes are carefully planned to meet the needs and interests of both the member company and the candidate. The Group also plans some 'reverse' attachments from member companies to government departments. On completion of their attachment, candidates write a report for their companies.

Seminars and Conferences

Each year the Group runs a number of seminars and conferences in response to requests and suggestions from members.

The company conferences are high level events which aim to provide up-to-date information about developments in the UK Civil Service and the EEC. They offer an opportunity for groups of senior business executives to hear, and discuss, reports from top civil servants.

Seminars are also held for candidates who have recently taken part in the attachment programme to enable them to share experiences and lessons learned.

For further details, contact:
The Whitehall and Industry Group
Claire Arnold 071-487 2621/Miranda Chalk 071-487 2623
Room C253, Michael House, 47 Baker Street, London W1A 1DN
Fax: 071-487 2622

Index